Executive Mother

Jill Parkin has her own page in the *Daily Express*
every Wednesday. Born and educated in Leeds,
she now lives in Sussex with her husband, David, and
their daughter, Rosie.

Executive Mother

Jill Parkin

Hodder & Stoughton
LONDON SYDNEY AUCKLAND

British Library Cataloguing in Publication Data

Parkin, Jill
Executive Mother
I. Title
306.874

ISBN 0-340-57610-3

Published by Hodder and Stoughton,
a division of Hodder and Stoughton Ltd,
Mill Road, Dunton Green,
Sevenoaks, Kent TN13 2YA
Editorial Office: 47 Bedford Square,
London WC1B 3DP

Photoset by Rowland Phototypesetting Ltd,
Bury St Edmunds, Suffolk

Printed in Great Britain by
Clays Ltd, St Ives plc

For my mother and father, Eileen and Leslie

Contents

1

Executive Mothers: Who we are and why we do it

It may not feel like it when you open your briefcase and find a pop-up picture book stuck by something indescribable to your conference notes, but you're part of a social revolution. You've had a long spell in a career, and now you've had a baby and you've decided to carry on with your career. This may be for one of several reasons, but no matter why you're doing it, you belong to a substantial and growing group. Sometimes it seems as if society hasn't yet come to grips with us. There is still precious little state help with childcare and there is still ambivalence about what we call working mothers. But we are undeniably here.

Women are choosing to start their families later than ever before. By the year 2000, 40 per cent of all babies will be born to women over 30. And maybe then our elderly female relatives will stop muttering about 'leaving it too late'. The trend is most marked in the professional middle classes, where the Executive Mother is becoming the norm, choosing to have children after ten or 15 years in a career. The birthrate among women in their twenties is lower than at any time since 1945. And after having the baby, nearly half of all working women return to work within nine months, twice as many as ten years ago. In the professional managerial classes, that figure is 60 per cent, double again. It's a sudden and marked social change. Women now are more likely than ever before to return to full-time work without loss of status. They're important at work because they're occupying ever more senior posts. They're important at home because they have salaries to match their husbands' or partners' salaries.

Widespread and fast, the trend leaves us struggling to adapt family and working life to each other. With any luck, this book helps to show how it can be done. That's certainly what I, a career veteran but a novice in the maternity stakes, set out to do. Sadly, there's been more progress on women's working front than on our domestic front. For most of us, having it all still means doing it all. The role of women has been changing rapidly and it's not easy to take a detached view of something you're part of, but there's no doubt that women need to help themselves negotiate this dual role. Otherwise we end up as economic or political pawns – told to work and given a little encouragement in the way of maternity legislation or provision when the nation is short of talents and skills and shoved back in the home and family role when not needed outside.

Why has the change shown in those figures happened? No doubt we've all been moved about the economic chessboard to a certain extent by other forces while fondly imagining we're moving under our own steam. But other factors have been at work to make our generation so different from our mothers' generation, so many of whom gave up work on marriage, let alone childbirth. Many of us can look back to our early years and remember our mothers, maybe our age now or probably younger, firmly based in the home. I remember coming home from school any time up to the age of ten or so to find civilised tea parties going on – my mother and two or three other mothers chatting in the sitting room. I remember patent leather shoes, cream-filled brandy snaps and everything winding up in time for my father's and their husbands' return from work.

But the change was already under way. Within a few years, those women were taking up part-time jobs, being in fact the forerunners of their career-minded daughters. There were changes in the mysterious world of taxes, National Insurance and pensions. Maternity rights came in. Sex discrimination became illegal. Women appeared in government. Painfully slowly, it's true, but they were in the public eye: role models before the phrase was coined. The number of places in higher education taken by women began to edge nearer the 50 per cent mark. We, the women of today's professional middle classes, were at school and careers were as much a part of our future as of our brothers' futures.

Life also became more expensive, with rampant consumerism and a flood of goods to be bought. Gradually, the stigma of having a wife who 'went out to work', as the phrase was, became rather mollified by the second salary. With inflation, a double garage and a lifestyle to keep up, it often became a necessity and it still is today.

It wasn't as simple as that. Women wanted a life outside the home too. Women wanted to work, not only to work but to have careers. Choice became the buzzword: about careers, marriage, motherhood and housewifery. Many women, of course, would argue we still don't have real choice and won't have it until there's better state provision for childcare in the way of tax relief or nurseries, but the possibility of being more than just a mother, more than just a childless worker, became real, even though it meant sacrifices as well as increased personal satisfaction. The Pill had brought another form of choice with it too. No doubt a convenience for men as well, it still gave women the power to choose when to have their children, to control their fertility.

So women today have many reasons for having children late. Among those figures quoted earlier are women having second families (around 70 per cent of divorce petitions come from women today); economically secure and independent women deciding to have a baby without the support of a man; women who have tried for many years and benefited later in the day from new fertility techniques. But the biggest group are the working mothers. And within that group are the Executive Mothers – the professionals who decide to do both. With more than one in 12 babies now born to women over 35, this is more than a matter of couples waiting and saving until they can afford a baby without sacrificing foreign holidays or fitted kitchens. This is women choosing to establish themselves and achieve well in a career before taking a break for planned motherhood. In England and Wales in 1989 there were 49,465 births to women aged 35 to 39 and 8,845 to women between 40 and 44. Many of them are career women.

The babies they have are wanted and planned babies, whose mothers have had years of independence and fulfilment and find that now is the time for children. Instead of feeling trapped by motherhood, they walk into it through choice and find it isn't a trap after all. They're less likely to feel resentful, because they've had a fair crack of the whip already. For years executive woman has had the money and freedom to enjoy her spare time as she wants: at the theatre, on holiday, in the gym, with her partner. Spending it with a baby or growing child instead is just another choice to make. And many professional women find they have the space in their lives when they reach their thirties.

One of our Executive Mothers said:

'If I were 22 and in the house day in day out with a toddler throwing food and paint around the place, I'd be a bitter, bad mother. As it is, I've had 15 years more than that 22-year-old to please myself and the last thing I want to do in my spare time is go to a night-club. To me, my baby daughter is an unqualified delight, no matter where the paint and the lamb dinner end up. Of course, I have the added luxury of knowing that in the morning, or after the weekend, I go back to work and it's the nanny's T-shirt which is being splattered. That helps me keep things in proportion too, I must admit. But the main thing is that I feel I've had some life of my own, my selfish time, if you like to put it that way.'

When it comes to looking at the nitty-gritty of handling a hostile employer or choosing between a nanny and a childminder, it's much more useful to examine how real women have coped than to consider how this famous woman or that chose to handle it. But at the same time, some experiences are common to us all, so in this chapter a few well-known women talk about various aspects of motherhood, completely at random.

Sally O'Sullivan, editor of *Good Housekeeping*, interviewed in the *Sunday Times* magazine in 1990, when she was 41, editor of *Harpers and Queen*, and her two children were eight and four.

The only time I get up really early, like 5 a.m., is when I have some writing to do – it's the only time to work undisturbed. At 5.10 I'm at the word processor. Then there's the hideous hour from 7.30 to 8.30, getting the children ready for school and us ready for work. My nanny starts around 8.30 – I feel I should do the mother bit at the beginning of the day. I'm always incredibly impressed with those working mothers who talk about having quality time with their children. I'm afraid my children have no idea what quality time is – in the mornings anyway. I'm always trying to snatch a newspaper, a cup of tea and then immediately a cup of black coffee.

I can usually get away from the office between six and seven for another bout of non-quality time with the children. The single most important thing is that when I open the door in the evening I hear my children roaring with laughter. Judy has been our nanny for seven years. She used to live in and I'm extremely lucky she's still with me now she's married. The children adore her. That is your whole freedom – someone you can trust.

But isn't it risky to leave motherhood late? Isn't it difficult to conceive and aren't you likely to produce an abnormal child? As we'll see in the medical chapter later on, reports of the difficulties facing the elderly primigravida have been greatly exaggerated, a fact proved by the statistics themselves. And with all the tests and treatments around today, the tick of the biological clock is fainter than it was. Older career women tend to be from higher socio-economic groups and so to be in better general health anyway. Dr John Collee, writing in the *Observer* colour supplement, put it very succinctly: 'From the obstetrician's point of view, a healthy woman of 38 is less of a risk than an unhealthy woman of 28.'

Actress Lindsay Duncan, in 1991, when she was 40 and six months pregnant with her first child.

> *I'm not worried about my age. It's hardly extraordinary these days, particularly for actresses. We're all piling up the work before taking time out. I'm conditioned to the idea of older mothers – my mother had me, her first child, just before her thirty-eighth birthday. I couldn't be happier about the timing of it. But I do try to stop thinking about me at the age of 50 and waiting at the school gates.*

And, of course, executive women tend to marry later than others. We're still in education and professional training, followed by promotion-hunting, while others are husband-hunting. The stimulation and demands of a career mean settling down early is not very attractive. There's too much going on and, being blunt, we're probably too selfishly involved in our own affairs. Two people can't move round the country together for the sake of two separate careers. And women with careers tend to develop and grow. At 35, you're not the person you were at 22 and heaven help both of you if you married then.

Economically, doing it late makes sense. You've got the money to take much of the stress out of raising a family. You can better afford the baby clothes and equipment, the childcare, the baby-sitters. And the children benefit from having parents who are more stable and less restless than many in their twenties who feel they haven't yet achieved anything for themselves. While talking to Executive Mothers, I was struck by their fascination and interest in their children. They seemed less likely than other women to take them for granted, as just an inevitable part of life.

Margaret Thatcher, writing in the *Sunday Graphic* in 1952, three months after her marriage. Her twins, Carol and Mark, were born the next year.

> *I hope we shall see more and more women combining marriage and a career. Prejudice against this dual role is not confined to men. Far too often, I regret to say, it comes from our own sex . . .*
>
> *Why have so few women in recent years risen to the top of the professions? One reason may be that so many have cut short their careers when they marry. In my view this is a great pity. For it is possible to carry on working, taking a short leave of absence when families arrive and returning later. In this way gifts and talents that would otherwise be wasted are developed to the benefit of the community. The idea that the family suffers is, I believe, quite mistaken. To carry on with a career stimulates the mind, provides a refreshing contact with the world outside – and so means that a wife can be a much better companion at home. Moreover, when her children themselves marry, she is not left with a gap in her life which so often seems impossible to fill.*
>
> *I should like to see married women carrying on with their jobs, if so inclined, after their children are born.*

Many Executive Mothers wish that Baroness Thatcher had suited her action to her words, by introducing tax relief for childcare when she was Prime Minister.

Today's middle-class professional women are less likely to settle for lower-paid part-time work after having their children. The training's done, the career's there, the right to return to your job after maternity leave is there. Why settle for pin-money? You can use your skills and income to set up a support system to help you, your partner and your baby. There's no particular formula for doing this, as I discovered while working on this book. Each couple copes with it differently.

Anita Roddick, of The Body Shop, writing for this book.

> *I had the career because I had the kids. I had my first baby when I was 26, my second at 28. The Body Shop wouldn't exist if I hadn't needed to scare up some source of income to support us all while my husband Gordon fulfilled his long-time dream of journeying from Buenos Aires to New York on horseback.*
>
> *The differences kids make to your life are always fundamental. Kids provide a sense of continuity. They make you responsible, and therefore more human, and they kick you into another generation, which is*

always good for the soul. But a working woman with children is in the most vulnerable of situations. They are her Achilles' heel, especially if she has no other support system. When they're ill, you don't work. When they're upset, you can't work.

I was lucky. Being Italian, I had a big extended family. That's how I survived. So I would always say that if you can, you should use your family to look after and love your children while you're working. Or find jobs that you're allowed to bring your kids to. Gordon and I originally ran a hotel – we turned our home into a source of income. I've mentioned Gordon a couple of times. I think that ultimately he held the key to the success of my particular situation. We have always shared everything – and I mean everything.

Time after time, career women stressed how important their partners had been to the whole enterprise. Not that all the women I spoke to were married to 'New Men', who can change a nappy, make a meal and still not suffer a virility crisis. I am, but that's just luck. Yet many did mention men who were pleased to be more involved with their children than their fathers were and, in the case of second-time-around fathers, to be more involved than they had been with their first family. All of which is a help if you decide to stick with your career through motherhood. But, of course, there's the other way of looking at it too.

Why do career women want babies? It seems to be a question without an answer. A career is no substitute for a baby, any more than a baby is for a career. And most women seem to want both. As we all know, there are women who choose to remain childless, or, as they would probably prefer to put it, childfree. But in spite of the difficulties, many women want both briefcase and babies, however single-minded they may appear at work. A colleague passed on to me a remark my immediate boss had made to the effect that he didn't believe that I could be interested in having children. In fact, unknown to both of them, I was already pregnant and had trouble suppressing the smirk.

Actress Julie Walters, writing for this book.

I had Maisie because the time was right – it just felt right. I felt I had something to give and life felt ever so slightly pointless before. It was also a good time in my career: I'd done most things I wanted to, I suppose. It has made a massive difference to our lives. Mine now has a point. Work is secondary and the main thing is I now feel I have a vulnerable heart – I'm not sure I did before.

> *Coping with work is very hard. I think if you decide to continue your career you have to make sure you really have decided. Otherwise you're utterly torn between home and work, a recipe for misery. Having Maisie is the very best thing I've ever done.*

Discovering your vulnerable heart does require some adjustment to the self-image. A teacher of French whom I met in the coffee lounge of a hotel in Sussex was doing what all mothers end up doing at some stage – sniffing her baby's bottom to assess whether she needed changing. 'You don't think after a while. You just do it, regardless of where you are,' she said. And, having got used to hauling up my T-shirt anywhere and everywhere to feed my own daughter, I understood just what she meant. Weekend shopping was all around, spilling out from the tray under the baby's pram. Her husband was sorting everything out, while she attended to the baby. All quite normal, but as she sniffed, she caught sight of the waitress coming to take her order. It was one of her sixth-form pupils on Saturday duty. The girl was quite unfazed at the sight of her head of French nappy-sniffing, but the teacher herself was rather confused. 'Teaching is partly about acting, keeping up an organised front. I feel as if I'd been caught out somehow,' she said.

Life is never as simple again once you've taken motherhood and career on board, but actually, whatever the transient disorder around you, you're really exercising more management skills than before. Now you have to fit in the school sports day, the baby's vaccinations and not forget to talk to the nanny about her boyfriend problem, as well as work. Your partner needs more than just the occasional bit of attention, too.

Comedian Victoria Wood, who did in fact manage to 'squeeze another one in' at the age of 38, interviewed for this book.

> *I always wanted to do it. I had Grace when I was 35 and I manage fine. I've a live-in, well, a live-round-the-corner nanny. Grace travels with me a lot, though I didn't take her to Ethiopia and I'm not taking her to the Bahamas. She stays at home with Dad. Don't forget the dads: they're crucial.*
>
> *I'm a babyaholic. I'm 38 now so I've just got time to fit another one in. You need a lot of energy, but if you're well and fit, you find it. Grace went on tour with me when she was just 18 months old and I did it myself, I carried all the luggage and the baby. I fed her and put her to sleep, then I did the show at night. I'm not one of those people who say: 'Oh, my nanny does it all.'*

What the baby wants is a happy mother. You have to be sensible about it and you have to pick your moment. Having children wouldn't have been a good idea when I was younger, trying to make it, dashing about, with no money. I'm only happy if I can do some work, but I've cut it down and do less now. I think you have to put them – the children – first and then put yourself a very close second, because if you're not happy, the baby isn't.

I'm lucky of course in that I can cut down the work, can afford the nanny. I'm very privileged. I would say to a working woman: 'You need stacks of energy, but if you're fit and strong, do it!'

There's another mental adjustment to be made, too, and it can start the very first time you go to your GP because you think you're pregnant. From being used to shouldering responsibility and knowing exactly what you're doing, you go straight into being a novice, and a mature novice at that. After all, we're always reading that obstetrically an older woman is someone over the age of 24. There can be a feeling of something else – the medical professionals – taking over and your own confidence can disappear.

It's rather a shock. But, as we see in a later chapter, Executive Mothers are often the best equipped to talk sensibly to doctors, midwives and obstetricians because they're older and better educated than many of the mothers these professionals are used to dealing with. You haven't got their specialised knowledge, but there's no reason why you should feel helpless because of it. In fact, the marriage between maternity and maturity has a lot going for it.

Actress Patricia Hodge, talking to the *Daily Express* weeks before the birth of her second son, when she was 45. She and her husband tried for 12 years before Patricia had her first baby at 43.

What I really can't believe is that this has happened to me second time around. And neither can my doctor. I felt the sort of joy you can hardly allow yourself to feel, the sort you can't talk about in case things go wrong. We were three weeks into filming The Cloning of Joanna May *when I discovered I was pregnant. I had the amniocentesis test and not until I'd gone through everything and was nearly six months pregnant did I tell a soul.*

Miraculous as it is, it's not the ideal time from the point of view of energy. At 40 your life is more complicated. You've filled up all the places which should have been taken up with children. You can take a backward step, but people don't like it if you suddenly try to de-complicate. My friends have been wonderfully supportive, but on a day-to-day basis you don't touch base the way you used to. Your whole life revolves around the small people. Even if you are working, the child comes first and that changes everything. When Alexander was born, he became the sole focus of my life, until I opened it up a bit.

I couldn't care less whether age is creeping up. It's these small people that matter. If a child turns round and says, 'Mummy, will you read me a story?' I have no choice. If it's the last thing on earth I have time to do, there is no way I could ever say no.

2

Professional and Personal: When to have a baby and what happens when you do

The truth is brutal: there's never a good point in your career to have a baby. But some times are better than others and, for most women, picking their moment is an exercise in damage limitation. Some women, of course, welcome changes motherhood brings to their working lives, but that's for later chapters.

Rowena, a City analyst, said:

'If Greg could have had the baby, it would have made far more sense. In my firm, people come and go all the time, there's a lot of movement, a lot of potential for promotion, a lot of head-hunting by outside firms. Being out of circulation really counts in the City: just reading the *Financial Times* on the sofa at home isn't enough. You're soon forgotten about if you're not in there, hustling. So, for me it was quite a wrench, not because I didn't want a baby as much as I wanted my job, but because I knew I might as well stick a sell-by date on my stomach.

'But Greg's job is different. He's with an insurance company. It's quite good money by many people's standards, but it's quite a lot less than I earn and frankly he finds the job rather boring and routine. He really lives for the weekends and for his squash nights. It was something he went into straight after university when the priority was to get a job and he's never been excited about it. Both personally and financially, it would have been better if he'd been the one with the womb, especially as I had a rough first few months and lost quite a lot of work with morning sickness. The City isn't a place for a ten o'clock starter these days.'

In fact, Rowena did go back to her job, though with a different firm. She felt that, as she wanted to breastfeed, she might as well have a break of a year to do the job thoroughly and rejoin the throng later. She played it very straight and didn't take maternity leave, simply resigning on good terms at seven months' pregnant. She said:

'We could afford it and simply cutting loose was a lot less hassle than having return dates hanging over my head for months. We did think about Greg becoming a househusband, but decided resources wouldn't stretch quite that far and opted for a child-minder when Joshua was a year old.'

When to do it isn't just a matter of a good point in your career. It also has to be the right time for you and your partner to give up the high life, if such you lead, and become parents.

But let's look at the job first. It's your office and nobody knows it as well as you do, so any advice has to be pretty general. The chances are that as a career woman your pregnancy will be planned, with nothing but the vagaries of fertility to get in the way, though I did once work with a woman who accidentally got pregnant just the month before she and her husband meant to start trying.

So, if you have a rough idea that you'd like to get pregnant in a year or so, you might want to consider a general chat about prospects with your boss. I'm not suggesting that you let the cat, or the baby, out of the bag. In fact, I'd suggest keeping it quiet. But you need to take into account where you'd like to be before you have the baby and where you'd like to be afterwards. He (sorry about this 'he': English needs a neutral word) may have plans for you, ideas about you, which you may want to know, or to reinforce, or to change. And if he hasn't, it may not be a bad thing to give him some of yours.

Of course, you run the risk that he may ask you point-blank if you're thinking of having children and you will have to assess whether he's asking you this to be helpful. Unless you're pretty confident he is going to be helpful, be vague and say you're not thinking babies for some time. He doesn't know how long some time may be. Or simply say no. There's nothing to prevent you starting to think any time after you close the door behind you. And remember that any discrimination because of pregnancy or suspicion of pregnancy is sexual discrimination and illegal. Advice on sexual discrimination can be obtained from the Equal Opportunities Commission, whose address is in the back of the book.

Once you know where you are, take a look around you at where everyone else is. One woman I spoke to delayed her pregnancy when she found out her colleague, whose job rather overlapped with hers, was already pregnant. 'It sounds ruthless, but there had always been a danger, if times got lean, that one of the two posts would go. Her pregnancy secured me for a while and then, while she was on maternity leave, I got a promotion. So she was happy too, because she came back to her job without any hassle.'

If you know a post you really want is coming up, don't get pregnant. Not every boss would be as good as mine was: he gave me one of the best slots on Fleet Street even though he knew I was pregnant. Of course, I like to think he was shrewd as well as good!

You can't do much about other people's movements, of course, though if your boss is new, you might consider 'working yourself in' with him before throwing away your cap or pills. Obviously you're protected by your maternity rights, but a boss isn't going to promote you or even think about someone he hardly knows who is on maternity leave. Of course, if you endlessly guard against every risk by putting pregnancy off, you'll eventually run out of time, men, or desire to have a baby at all. It's a risk we all take. But sometimes we don't realise we're taking it.

A friend of mine was a keen marathon runner. She and her husband, especially her husband, were very keen to have children. But Julia kept putting it off from one year to the next, because there were always marathons to train for and to run in. She would come home from work, change straight into her running gear and head for the moors around her home in the Peak District of Derbyshire. She was so keen, her husband felt ground down by it.

'I don't mind the rain at all,' she said to me. 'Once you're really soaked, right through to your knickers, it doesn't matter. I run and run until I reach a high and then I run and run some more.' She struck me as an exercise addict, but then most people who do more than walk to and from the station every day strike me as that. A day without taking to the hilly tracks left her physically low and irritable.

Then she found out she had endometriosis, which you're more liable to get if you ovulate regularly and put off pregnancy. She was warned this could mean infertility and reacted by deciding she didn't want children really: she just wanted to be fit for the next marathon. This caused problems and a temporary separation from her husband.

She went along to the British Pregnancy Advisory Service 'just to confirm it, to get clear in my head that I couldn't have children, so I could accept it and get on with the rest of my life.' There she was told that at least half the women with the dreaded endometriosis can have children and she rethought things. She and her husband got back together. She was 38 when she had her first baby and 40 when she had the second. It wasn't the job which made her delay, but it could have been. Having said all that, see the medical chapter for some reassurance on motherhood and age! By the way, the service Julia used is no longer offered by the BPAS, who are referring women with infertility problems to Issue, whose services I describe fully in Chapter 4, page 40.

It's no good considering your job in isolation; there's your partner's work, too. You'll want him around for you and the baby, not travelling the globe being too young and thrusting. So talk about his job, too. If you didn't have to face it when you began your relationship, there's also the question of whose job the pair of you will follow around once you have a baby. Will you decide on money grounds or on who spends most time with the child? If he's got a promotion coming up, it could be financially a good time to have a baby. If he's in a precarious position, then it may not be, unless yours is well shored up with decent maternity terms. Like the costs of childcare, timing is a joint thing.

And now to that high life. I wouldn't have said, before our daughter was born, that David and I led a high life, but in retrospect it sometimes seems as if we did. With a young baby, it is easy to get to the point where a night out at the theatre makes you one of life's ravers.

Very soon after Rosie was born, we were invited to a wedding. The invitation said: 'Followed by rock and roll party.' Not many three-day-old babies can rock 'n' roll and the same can be said for their parents' social life. I stayed at home. My husband looked in for a short while and left as the first few notes of 'Blue Suede Shoes' came drifting in from the dance room, reflecting that life had changed for ever.

About ten years earlier, when I was living by myself in my own flat and inclined to throw the odd party, I hardly had a clue as to what life could be like with children. Then a couple of close friends, who went on to have four babies in five years, turned up with a carrycot – the first time such a thing had happened at one of my parties – and a two-year-old. The little boy was put to sleep in my bed, blissfully unaware of the mounting pile of coats around him. To my horror, my friends said going out was a rare event these days. They tended to ask people round rather than accept invitations. I vaguely wondered if there was a national dearth of babysitters, but of course I didn't understand. Didn't understand that you don't want to hand over a newborn baby to the girl next door, that the worry will ruin the evening, that life changes.

I remember, while waiting for my overdue baby, looking longingly at the advert for a Judi Dench–Kenneth Branagh production of *Coriolanus* a few weeks later. I would have loved to see it, but there were no potential babysitters on hand – as a commuter I hardly knew any people in the town where we lived, certainly no one I knew well enough to trust and ask to babysit. If you're used to doing things on a whim, whether they're for work or pleasure, it comes as quite a shock to find the simplest things in your life need planning, even a trip to the swimming pool. A dash to the sales with a baby requires strict discipline: one store too many and your entire operation is ruined by a wet, hungry and unhappy child and a lot of tut-tutting assistants. And it's the smallest thing in your life and in your household which has taken everything over. Babies eat time. For a couple used to a lot of socialising, adjusting to the needs of a baby can be difficult.

Explaining why he wouldn't give in to his girlfriend's request for children, one of my male colleagues said:

'I can see it stretching before me. Dinner in front of the television every night. If I want to play sport on Saturdays I'll be made to feel guilty because she'll be going round the supermarket with the baby. No more easy weekends in Paris or Amsterdam just because we feel like it. What do you do if you suddenly want to see a film? Put it in your Filofax for two weeks on Tuesday when you think you might be able to get a babysitter? You can't just jump in the car and go, can you? And when they're older, you're nothing but a glorified taxi service. You can't let children run loose these days, you know. They'll get knocked down or molested. It's a full-time job and I've got one of those already.'

One of the pluses of it all, though, is the realisation other couples are doing the same thing. You may not be able to accept those last-minute invitations to drinks which turn out to be midnight restaurant sessions. But other sorts of socialising take their place. Sunday lunch (bring your carrycot and put it next to ours) is a favourite among couples who share the same restrictions of babies or young children. It can be a bit clubby, offputting is how one of my childless friends put it, but when you feel as if you haven't been out for months, sitting conspiratorially round someone else's pile of soft toys for a change feels like a treat.

Once you're back at work, social life depends on the arrangements you've made for childcare, of course. But the chances are you'll want to spend a good part of the time you're not working with your baby, whether or not you have the energy to make it 'quality time'.

If you feel you'd resent the restriction on your freedom, then you don't need telling to think twice before getting pregnant. A 33-year-old colleague of mine, with remarkable honesty, told me at an office party she 'wasn't ready to stop impressing men yet'. What her husband thought of that, and why it should stop with motherhood anyway, I don't know. But he wasn't keen on children yet either because, she said, he was still into the 'whole lifestyle bit, making money and spending it'. She did see the funny side of it all and, just for good measure, she added that one of her reasons for wanting children eventually was to have someone to inherit everything they hadn't already spent. All very odd, but a lesson on how important it is to acknowledge your priorities before you embark on something which, or somebody who, willy-nilly has to come first. Actually, remembering this conversation now, I realise my daughter was just six weeks old at the time. Perhaps I was an object lesson for my colleague that motherhood meant not being impressive to men . . .

As a high-earning couple used to socialising, you'll find things very different, but you might actually find it's a relief to be off the social circuit for a while. A baby can be good company as well and probably more fun than a lot of the people you run into at parties.

One important thing, though. After-work drinks and the like disappear, but don't write off really important social affairs to do with work just because you have to have your quota of time with your baby. There aren't likely to be that many social functions and yours are unlikely to coincide with your partner's, so say yes to that special invitation. It's important to be seen in circulation and to give the lie to any impression that motherhood has taken over your life to the extent of affecting your dedication to work. Oh, and don't be guilt-ridden about it: your baby won't suffer.

On my maternity leave, I went to my editor's birthday party, leaving my precious breastfed daughter with her father and a bottle. She was rather tearful when I went to catch my train. When I reached the office, I rang home straight away: she'd fallen asleep shortly after I'd left, just five minutes into a European Cup football match. How like her mother.

At the party I was worried equally about whether she was crying over her bottle and whether my breast pads were up to the strain. I rang home from the station. Oh, the guilt! 'I wish you'd stop ringing,' said my husband. 'You'll wake the baby.' No chance. She finally woke, just as I turned my key in the lock, after a five-hour sleep and in time for a feed before bed.

The other change to your life, whatever arrangements you make for childcare, is which of you takes the greater share of looking after the baby at other times. In other words, who takes time off when she is ill or needs her vaccinations or, in later years, has music exams? You don't want to leave everything up to the nanny and these things just aren't part of a childminder's duties. If you're both equal professionals, then you're both equal parents too. Don't fall into the same trap which ensnares so many women with house-work. You notice the windows need cleaning. He doesn't. So you clean them. You notice the baby's nails need cutting or that she has a rash. And of course in the end you're the one rushing round and working in your leisure time. Share all the duties. Anticipate them and if necessary come to some agreement about who bathes the baby, who reads the toddler a bedtime story. That way you have time for each other, too.

More than one Executive Mother has fixed her maternity leave, had her baby and then hit a problem with her partner. Some men, even Executive Fathers who are used to two incomes, find it hard to accept that their wives still consider their work is import-ant and probably every bit as important as a man's work.

A deputy head of personnel had a surprise when she discussed childcare with her husband.

'I hadn't realised what a mummy's boy he was. After the baby was born, any slight problems we had he always found a way of mentioning to his mother, who actually was wise enough not to be too heavy with the advice. But before that, he kept saying how she'd stayed at home to bring him and his sister up and how that was the best thing for the child. I said I wouldn't be happy at home all day and that I didn't want to lose my independence. His response to that was that children were a choice after all. As you know, that argument can go back and forth for ever.

'It was only when we sat down together and worked out the money that he realised the difference it would make to our lifestyle if I didn't go back. It really surprised him when I said we'd have to think about the weekly grocery bill. There'd be no more blitzing Sainsburys on a Saturday without looking at the prices and no more buying wine without really thinking about it. Our joint health-club membership would have to go, too. The cost of a childminder was about a quarter of what I brought home. He reluctantly accepted that but then tried to talk me into going part-time, which I point-blank refused to do.

'I just went ahead. I set up the childcare and simply took it for granted that I was going back to work normally. It worked, but he still has this unshakeable assumption that I will work outside the home and do most things with the baby as well. He just assumes I'll drop her off on my way to work and pick her up at the end of the day, that I'll take time off when she's ill. Of course, that's just what happens. He's very good at the nice things: singing to her, bathing her, but he soon gets bored. Motherhood has been an eye-opener about marriage for me.'

When I mentioned this book to a woman I know who teaches piano in her own home, she pointed out another difficulty for the Executive Mother.

'Before we had Emma, if a job in another town had cropped up for one of us, we'd have decided on grounds of money, prospects, etc., whether we accepted it and moved, knowing that the other would have to find another job. Lawrence and I both taught in the same college and I'd gone back to teaching without a problem when Emma was six months old.

'Then he was offered a departmental headship somewhere else. There was a token discussion of it, but I felt he'd really made up his mind to accept it. It meant more money for him and I went along with it, thinking I'd find another post eventually. In his eyes, and I think in mine, the importance of my job had somehow diminished with motherhood. So we moved and there was no job available for me the first year. We hadn't found a childminder either. So while we waited for both I started taking pupils at home and looking after Emma myself. I found a playgroup for her three mornings a week.

'Of course, it became a habit, our lifestyle, in fact. It's quite pleasant and being at home certainly made things easier with the second pregnancy. Then I had to shift all my pupils to the evenings so Lawrence could look after the children until James was old enough for the playgroup too.

'I suppose I am still a working mother, but I don't know whether I'd fit into your Executive Mother book other than as a warning. I've no prospect of promotion in this job and it will be two or three years before James is at school and I can even think of another post. Somehow in our relationship we lost the job equality. I'm not saying I was reduced to pin-money, but I definitely slipped into second place.'

Apart from the change in the relationship the two of you have, there's another relationship which often affects the career woman embarking on motherhood. Many of us have no children of our own but have married some step-children, as it were. The arrival of half-brothers and sisters is going to affect them whether they live with you or, as is more likely, with their mother. These things seem entirely unpredictable. Their reception of your news may be better than you ever hoped or worse than you feared. When my husband's 17-year-old came to visit the new baby for the first time, she bounded into the hall saying: 'Where's my sister?' I've rarely been so relieved in all my life.

One Executive Mother-to-be had a similar experience with the twin 15-year-old girls from her husband's first marriage.

'I was rather worried because of what had happened before. The girls live with their mother nearby and they stay with us every other weekend. Like any of these arrangements, it has its stresses, mainly my feeling irritable sometimes that I can't have John to myself. But I knew what I was taking on when we started living together and by and large it worked very well. The girls didn't seem to see me as a rival to their mother. After all, I arrived on the scene well after the divorce and to them I seemed so much involved with my career that I think the possibility of our having children had really never dawned on them. I also think, knowing how I felt when I was their age, that I seemed far too old to have children – well into my thirties, for heaven's sake, the same age as their mother and she was really old. You know the sort of thing.

'Anyhow, we had a good relationship all the time John and I were living together and then all hell broke loose when we announced we were getting married. We told them quite casually, the pair of them, asking how they'd like to be treated to two new dresses and what were they doing on such and such a date. It was a low-key registry affair and hotel lunch, no big deal, and I suppose we expected them to take it in the same low-key way. What was the real difference between living together and getting married? Surely it was just a romantic gesture?

'Apparently it was a lot more than that to them. They both looked as if we'd hit them with a sledgehammer, burst into tears and disappeared for a long walk. They missed Sunday lunch altogether. When they came back, they tried to talk about it, but couldn't really explain it and kept saying sorry, which was rather upsetting, because I did feel it was our fault, not theirs. They got over it in a few weeks and happily came along to the wedding. They never said so, but I think that what was at the back of their minds was that some day, somehow their parents would get back together again. I suppose that, no matter how good their relationship is with the "other woman", at heart all children feel that.

'So, you can imagine how I was dreading telling them we were expecting a baby. We hadn't ever discussed it with them, because I really didn't see why I should ask anyone's permission, except my husband's, to get pregnant. So, as they were his children, I played the coward and left him to tell them while I was away one weekend. We'd left it as late as we could before the bulge gave us away. Like me, John was expecting the worst. He practically had the tissues at his elbow. They were actually fine, really good about it. They had thought of it once we got married, it turned out.

'By the next visit they were positively keen, which I think showed that their mother had given out the right signals about it. One wanted a boy, the other wanted a girl. They rather hoped, because the dates were pretty close, that the baby would be born on their birthday. I couldn't believe it. They wanted to see what babyclothes I'd bought and went quite soppy over them. They apparently talked about the new baby at school and, when I was still pregnant after my due date, they were ringing up almost daily to find out what was happening. They were more impatient than I was. John's mother said she'd expected that all along. "Girls love babies" was her simple explanation and maybe she's right.

'Afterwards, they were very keen for me to play the traditional mum role. One of them even asked if I would be glad to give up work. In the event, because of problems at work, I did stop for a while, which they obviously thought was right. I think they would have seen anything else as a criticism of their mother and the way they were brought up. They rather raised their eyebrows when I did go back to work eighteen months later and we acquired a nanny. Of course, it was me, not John, they looked askance at. But by then they loved the baby so much, it was all right. I'm looking forward, rather smugly, to what they have to say about who should look after baby when they're launched on their own careers and start feeling that maternal urge.'

One woman I talked to admitted frankly to a mixture of bribery and psychology.

'We took the children – a boy and a girl, ten and 13 – to Euro Disney for the weekend. They had a super time, so on the last afternoon I said: "And next year, when we all come again, we'll have a baby to bring." My husband looked appalled. He'd been dithering and dithering about how to tell them. He'd even suggested asking his ex-wife to tell them, which made me furious. I didn't see what it had to do with her or why she should be told at all by anyone but the children. I thought it was rather clever actually, because I instantly included them in the new family.

'They didn't quite take it in at the time and did a lot of talking to their father about it, but I considered that was his job. My only duty, if you like, was to tell them I still wanted them around and thought of them as part of our life. I considered I'd done that by making clear they were coming along next year. They were both rather cautious for a while and the girl was uncertain because the baby might be another daughter for daddy, but it all settled down eventually. You've got to do it. You can't let these things stand in your way. They'll grow up and do the same thing themselves, after all. And long before that, they have their own lives and their parents are no longer the centre of everything.'

For Jenny, who runs her own recruitment consultancy in Cheshire, the whole thing was rather a nightmare.

'My husband's always been keen to keep his ex-wife sweet for the sake of his daughter. She's the sort to pass everything on to her. She still refers to me as "that woman" even though we're married, so when Jessica goes home after the weekend she really can't talk about what we've done or where we've been. Michael

21

worries she might try to stop her coming. I've always had a problem with Jessica. She's very civilised and polite, but I know that if I'm not there for the weekend, which sometimes happens because of conferences and that kind of thing, it's the icing on the cake for her. She has her beloved daddy to herself. I understand how she feels, but sometimes I wish she'd blow a gasket with me so we could have it out.

'She took it like a lamb when Michael very gently broke it to her, but the same night his ex-wife was on the phone in a neurotic state, blaming "that woman" because Jessica was sobbing in her bedroom. She thought he should have told her first so she could decide whether Jessica should be told or whether it was a good thing for her to continue her visits if she had to share her father with another woman's child. It was bloody awful. I could hear her and I could hardly keep my hands off the phone. Jessica stopped coming. She thought her father wouldn't want her now he had a new baby. I don't think it was just because of the baby, but because she felt she owed a duty to her mother who was obviously still not clear what she felt for Michael and had made Jessica feel she had to look after her.

'Recently, when she stayed with us for part of a summer vacation, Jessica explained she'd felt abandoned, part of a failure, something which hadn't worked. She felt her mother had nobody, whereas we had each other and a baby, so she had to stick with her mother. She didn't come to stay for well over a year. It was a real blight on our baby's first few months and I felt, of course, horrendously guilty. Not only was I going back to work almost immediately (it's my own business) and leaving the baby with a childminder, but I'd screwed up my husband's relationship with his daughter. What sort of maternal feelings could I lay claim to on any grounds? Did he blame me?

'Michael decided to play it softly softly and not make any demands on Jessica. His first wife's reaction was very much: "Well, what could you possibly have expected? She feels ousted." I rather fancied she was the one who felt ousted. Then, without telling each other, we both wrote to Jessica on her birthday. There was no response until Michael's birthday when she told her mother she wanted to see her dad and take his present round. He was absolutely knocked out and she could see it. She stood long and hard looking at the baby, who was practically walking. It was fine after that. She was a lot better with me, too. The baby gave us something in common.'

There are other relationships for the Executive Mother to think about. Susie J., a university lecturer, was rather astonished by her mother's attitude.

'I couldn't believe it because she'd always been really interested in my career, in my research, all the exams I passed at school and later. She'd been supportive without being pushy. Then suddenly, when I announced I was pregnant, she started behaving as if this was my whole *raison d'être*, as if everything else in my life had just been time-passing until the great day I reproduced. Then one day I mentioned a conference in the States the following summer where I was delivering a paper and she said: "I suppose they'll easily find someone else. You'll be able to give them plenty of notice."

'She actually thought, assumed, I was taking four or five years off until the baby was old enough to go to school. I said I not only intended to go to America, but to return to work fairly soon after the birth. She was totally horrified. Then she said: "Well, I don't live near enough for you to leave the baby with me every day." I realised then what a huge gap there was between her generation and mine. Working mothers were part of a different world from hers. I explained about the crèche on campus and she said a stranger would be looking after my baby. I can't pretend that didn't hurt, even make me think for a minute. But the world has moved on since she was a mother. I was surprised by the whole thing, though. I never expected opposition from that quarter. She wasn't deliberately hostile, just disbelieving, which was actually harder to cope with.

'Even now she's almost wistful about things in Katy's development she thinks I might be missing. She comes out with things like: "I don't suppose you heard her first word" or "You'll have to ask at that nursery if she's playing with books yet." Silly things, but rather hurtful. I've tried telling her that it's better for the baby to have a happy and fulfilled mother rather than someone who's frustrated beyond belief by being at home all the time. I've also spelled out to her that we couldn't manage on just one salary anyway. She says families used to manage on just the man's earnings and it's not a matter of what you earn but what you spend. She's rather better on homilies than I am, so I just let her go on. I could say she was seeking to justify the way she lived, I suppose . . .'

Aren't we all? There's no single moral to be drawn from this chapter because all our jobs and relationships are different. But we've had a look at the pitfalls, so now let's be positive and look at how to handle your pregnancy at work and how to get the best deal you can.

3
Your Rights:
And fighting for more

It's not a secret that will keep. If your office is anything like mine, any woman under 50 is suspected of pregnancy if she so much as puts a medical appointment in the diary. Start turning your computer screen off when you're not actually using it and stop drinking the machine coffee and they're virtually applying for your job. Best to seize the initiative yourself before people start talking. And if you are working for a woman, don't automatically expect a sympathetic hearing. No boss, of either sex, will be glad you're pregnant.

If you can, morning sickness and early scares allowing, wait until you've passed the three-month mark before you tell your boss you are pregnant. Most miscarriages occur early on, long before there's any bulge to see. One in six women who know they are pregnant miscarry and only a quarter of all conceptions are thought to result in a live birth. Miscarriages are known to increase with maternal age. Waiting will also give you time to sort yourself out and decide what you want to do and find out what the options are. The last thing you want is people asking you what you plan to do about work when you've only just found out you're pregnant. Resist the temptation to confide in special colleagues – it's no advantage to you and the chances are they'll break the confidence. And watch your lunchtime shopping: it's hard to hide a sterilising kit, baby alarm and full set of Mister Men books in a handbag.

Not that things always go to plan, as I found out. An alarm early in my pregnancy meant taking a week off work, with doctor's orders to do nothing but sit or lie down. 'I don't want to bump into you in Safeway,' she warned. So, of course, although I only told my immediate boss, the office surmise machinery went into overdrive and by the time I returned to the office, at only nine weeks pregnant, there didn't seem much point in denying that I was pregnant.

Executive Women often know very little about maternity rights. We've had other things to think about. And hasn't legislation taken care of everything? Well, if that's right, what went wrong for Elaine Redding? Hers is just one of the several cases which make the news columns each year of a woman meeting hostility at work because of her pregnancy. Her boss told her to have an abortion or leave her job as team leader in a charity hostel in Oxford when she complained of morning sickness. Mrs Redding left. After her baby girl was born she won her claim of sexual discrimination at an industrial tribunal. Her compensation was £1,200.

Not a fortune, really, is it? It shows it's well worth finding out your rights before you break the glad tidings to your employer. It could be that you find you have the most enlightened boss around, who will encourage you to go to antenatal classes, will send flowers to the maternity ward and be generally thrilled for you. Or it could be that you find you haven't.

Tell your boss first, privately. Don't let him find out from other people or guess because you suddenly appear in what looks like his mother's sofa covers. He will appreciate being told first and being given good notice of your intentions. But go armed with all the information. The company handbook, if there is one, is a good start – there should be a section on maternity leave.

Susie, a university lecturer in geography, put off telling her boss she was pregnant until the day she had to cancel a morning seminar because of sickness.

'I thought, "Right, no more of this. I'd better own up." It really felt like that, as if I were confessing something. I had absolutely no idea of my rights, apart from that I was entitled to have my job back afterwards, so I walked in to see our professor unarmed. I'd had the job less than two years and had a vague idea he might think I'd deliberately timed it so I would just qualify for leave. It hadn't actually been like that at all. We'd simply stopped using contraception, thinking it might happen within the year and it happened straight away.

'Anyhow, I told him and he seemed totally astonished. Very pleased for me, but astonished. I suppose there aren't many women in my subject and we tend to be treated like honorary chaps anyway, so to find out one of his chaps was four months pregnant was rather a surprise. It was the first pregnancy he'd had to deal with as head of the department. He kept saying we would manage somehow and pointed out there was a campus crèche which would make things much easier. He was being very nice and very fatherly, but obviously the nitty-gritty of maternity leave and pay was completely out of his experience. I had to mention it in the end and he looked very worried and referred me to the Admin department.

'It actually worked out rather well, because I wanted to go on working as long as I could and he seemed to assume that I would. So we fixed another appointment and in the meantime I sorted everything out about leave and pay with the help of my union, the Association of University Teachers, and with the University personnel staff. So the second time I saw my professor, at least I knew what I was talking about. It turned out I was entitled to more than the minimum leave – 52 weeks in all, though I didn't take anything like it. His attitude all along was that it was something that could be worked round and that I was a valuable member of his staff. I was grateful for that.

'Had I wanted to milk the system for every last day of leave and had dozens of clinic appointments in University time he would probably have questioned my commitment, which he wouldn't have been entitled to do and which might have led to rows, but we were actually both rather assuming I would work late and stay in touch with everything while I was off. Mind you, he looked very crestfallen when I said I couldn't take the first year limestone field trip to the Yorkshire Dales, by which time I would have been six months pregnant.'

You need to know your rights, legal and in-house. Many companies offer a better deal than the legal minimum and we'll mention some of them later. And remember, these packages aren't fixed in stone. You're a valued employee, with considerable clout. Bargain for what you want. There are four main maternity rights: leave and reinstatement; statutory maternity pay; protection from dismissal owing to pregnancy; reasonable paid time off for antenatal care. The two main areas to be mastered at this stage are time off and pay. Get these dry facts and figures in your head before you tell all. You want to be in charge and knowing where you stand first gives you the upper hand. Here we go.

Maternity Leave

The first, and rather sobering, statistic is that in Britain only 60 per cent of pregnant working women are eligible for maternity leave. Women in Britain are much worse off than in other European countries, where leave is automatic regardless of whether you've worked any length of time for that employer. The knock-on effect of this is that in Sweden, for example, eight out of ten women return to work straight after maternity leave, compared to three out of ten in Britain. By nine months after the birth, nearly half of women in Britain who worked during their pregnancy are back at work. A high proportion are executive women.

Maternity Benefits

To qualify for leave, you must:

1. Have two or more years of continuous service with your present employer by the end of the twelfth week before the week the baby is due and to work at least 16 hours a week. Or, if the company's hours are fewer than 16 a week, you need to have five years' service by the end of the twelfth week before the week the baby is due and work at least eight hours a week. (Under a new deal worked out with the EC, not yet in force, women will be eligible for leave and 14 weeks' wages at a minimum of statutory sick pay as soon as they start work, rather than after two years. The new legislation must be brought in before October 1994.)

2. Give your employer written notice of your intention to return to work after the birth of the baby and to continue working until the eleventh week before the expected birth. You don't have to state your return date to work, though, until your baby is born.

3. If asked by your employer not earlier than 49 days after the expected week of confinement to do so, confirm in writing within 14 days your intention to return after the birth.

4. Give your employer at least three weeks' notice of your date of return. The company may well ask for a copy of your maternity certificate (Form MAT B1) which your midwife or GP will give you when you are about six months pregnant.

If you fulfil ALL these conditions you have the right to up to 40 weeks maternity leave beginning 11 weeks before the birth and finishing 29 weeks from the week of the birth. You can choose to work closer to the birth or return sooner.

You can't have more than 29 weeks leave unless one of these situations applies:

- You're ill, which means you can delay your return for four weeks. You must let your employer know that you are ill before the date you were to return and you must send in a medical certificate.
- Your employers can delay your return for four weeks, if they give you a reason and give you a new date for your return.

Maternity leave does not count as a break of service, so it doesn't affect pension rights, but other rights and perks may be affected and we'll look at those later in this chapter. Any general change in terms and conditions (annual pay rounds, cost of living rises and the like) will apply to you on your return to work. And, a very important point for those who want another child later: because leave counts as continued service, you don't have to wait another two years to qualify for leave for your next baby.

During the 1980s new rules were brought in which gave small employers, with fewer than six workers, the right not to reinstate a woman employed after maternity leave. And, more importantly for the executive woman, where it was not reasonably practicable for the employer to give the woman her original job, she could be offered reinstatement on 'terms and conditions not substantially less favourable'. None of which was good news for working women!

If you don't know whether you will want to go back to work, do everything as above and make up your mind finally when you need to tell your employer three weeks before the date of return.

Statutory Maternity Pay

There are three types of maternity pay, depending on how long you have worked for your present employer. Eighty per cent of women who work during pregnancy receive some form of maternity pay.

Basic Statutory Maternity Pay
You qualify for 18 weeks of SMP at the flat rate if you have six months' continuous insured employment with the same employer up to the fifteenth week before the expected week of confinement.

Higher rate SMP
You qualify for six weeks SMP at 90 per cent of your salary plus 12 weeks flat rate SMP if you have worked for 16 hours a week for two years (or between eight and 16 hours a week for five years) continuously with the same employer up to the fifteenth week before the expected week of confinement.

Maternity Allowance
Maternity Allowance comes from the state, not from the employer. You qualify for 18 weeks Maternity Allowance if you have six months insured employment or self-employment in the 12 months preceding the fourteenth week before the expected week of confinement.

An executive woman is unlikely to be eligible for Maternity Allowance, which is a social security payment for women who don't get SMP. (From April 1993, it's £43.75 a week for up to 18 weeks.)

From April 1993 the basic rate of SMP is £47.95 a week, paid for up to 18 weeks. To get it, you have to ask your employer for it in writing at least three weeks before you stop working. SMP can be paid for any 18-week period between week 11 before the birth and week 11 after the birth.

Of course, if you're fit you may want to work later in your pregnancy. If so, bear in mind that for every week you work after the seventh week before the birth you will lose one week's SMP (i.e. if you work in week six and start SMP in week five you can only get 17 weeks SMP). SMP is paid by the month, assuming that's how you are normally paid, and tax and National Insurance contributions will be deducted as usual.

Frances is a magazine journalist in London. She's 35 and has two children now.

'I thought, "This is going to be a doddle. What could be easier than telling a woman editor of a magazine which is forever running stories about the joys of parenthood that you're pregnant? She'll probably order the knitting editor to get going on the christening robe." Well, she didn't. She was fine about it, absolutely fine, but there was no mistaking that she thought the company was doing me a favour.

'She checked my service to the day, then and there, on the phone to the personnel department. She knew, not surprisingly with a nearly all-female staff, exactly the legal entitlement and she made it clear that was all there was. With so many women on the staff, they couldn't afford to be generous, was her line. And she said she wanted me to say in writing pretty smartly when I was starting my leave and when I would be back. And she told me to book my antenatal appointments well ahead and make sure they were in the diary. She was cool rather than actually hostile – extremely businesslike, even when she congratulated me.

'I got a formal letter spelling out what I could expect. It was the minimum. I had to return my company car the day I left for my leave. I couldn't amass holidays during my leave and my newspaper and telephone allowances would stop for the duration. It all seemed rather petty, but the older women at work, who had brought up their children long before there was any legislation for maternity leave and pay, made it clear they thought I should be grateful. Still, as all the younger mothers I worked with said, the company itself was very good in a formal sort of way, sending flowers to the hospital and a basket of baby things after the birth. But it was all obviously business as usual for them.'

Getting Over and Above the Statutory Minimum

You'll have realised the big snag by now – only 18 of the possible 40 weeks of leave are paid by law. Obviously, you and your partner will have to budget and think ahead for what will amount to a pretty hefty loss of earnings for a large part of a year. But you may be one of the luckier ones, with either better leave arrangements or better pay or even both. There's a huge variation. You may find your company offers full pay for at least the earlier part of maternity leave, or that you are allowed to keep your company car and other perks, like telephone expenses.

Check with your union, your employer or the personnel department to find out if there's a better package available. Whatever is on offer, get it in writing. The chances are that as a career woman, this wasn't one of the things you took into account when you joined your company. If you're like me, you never even read that part of the handbook! By the way, this is the point – actually, one of several points – where women working in the public sector score heavily.

When the Policy Studies Institute prepared its report on Maternity Rights in Britain, which was published in 1991, it found that 28 per cent of employers, largely in the public sector, had extended maternity rights and benefits over and above the statutory minimum. This wasn't philanthropy, but a response to severe staff shortages. They needed to attract mothers back to work.

Length of service

Some local authorities allow women with only one preceding year of service to qualify for leave. The Civil Service is best of all – one year's service during the last three years. Private sector companies which give maternity leave after one year include British Telecom, British Gas, Esso, Rowntree Mackintosh and Freeman's Mail Order. Some local authorities give part-time women the same rights as full-time. Allowing a longer break after the birth than the statutory 29 weeks is rather rarer, but British Telecom, on a discretionary basis, allows up to 18 months beyond the twenty-ninth week. The overall leave of 40 weeks has been increased to 52 weeks for university teachers, National Health Service employees, civil servants and employees of some London borough councils.

Maternity pay

It's top marks to the Civil Service again. They allow three months on full pay. Hammersmith Council offers 16 weeks full and 12 weeks half pay. In the private sector, there are a few (very few) examples of enhanced maternity pay, ranging from 20 on full and 20 on half pay to 13 on full and 16 on half pay.

Before you break the news to your boss, think of your job as a whole package, not just as time and money. Apart from your salary, what other things does your job bring you? Company cars, cheap car loans, mortgage subsidies/lower-rate mortgages and private health care are all major parts of the package, not to mention the smaller things such as having your phone and newspaper bills paid. Companies vary considerably in what they allow women to keep during maternity leave. Most insist on having the company car returned. Some allow loans to continue on the understanding that you return to work. Find out whether the company will continue to contribute to your pension during maternity leave – it's well worth bargaining for and getting confirmation in writing.

If necessary make a list of all these things. What they don't offer you, ask for. Remember that they want to keep your loyalty. They want you back. They don't want you to defect to another employer who will give you a better deal next time you want a baby. You're not begging; you're doing a deal.

But don't go in there with guns blazing: it needn't be a confrontation. When an organisation called Maternity Alliance did a nationwide survey among working mothers, 56 per cent said the reaction of the boss was good. Twenty-eight per cent reported a mixed response and 16 per cent a bad response. Mind you, women are so grateful for even a neutral acceptance of their news that they tend to class that as good. Assuming you intend to return to work, you must get your commitment to returning to work across to your boss. He needs to know where he is and will be grateful for your plain dealing.

When you've decided to tell your boss, you'll find the words yourself. There's no need to give a script here. But do make an appointment to break the news in private and get the thing off on a good footing. I've seen two women make their announcement as if they were in a Tennessee Williams play. One, head of her department, was arguing a case with her deputy in an open-plan office. 'Anyhow,' she said at full volume, 'I don't care! I'm pregnant and I mustn't be upset!' The other, weeping at her desk, simply stood up and said: 'I'm pregnant and I'm going home.' She did. Neither would have chosen that way, but their hormones got in there first. So, make that appointment and tell him yourself.

Say loud and clear that you want to be kept in touch with everything of importance. Say you would like key internal mail and company literature to be sent to you at home. If courses you would normally go on are being planned for after your likely return, or maybe even during your leave, you want to be included. The same goes for conferences. Don't tell these things only to your boss: he may find the enthusiasm commendable, but he's unlikely to do anything about it himself. Tell the secretaries, the PAs and others who fix these things and ask them to send copies of any memo to your boss to confirm the arrangements.

Many pregnant women find they are no longer considered worthy of investment and discover training courses are mysteriously cancelled. One advertising executive in the Maternity Alliance survey said, 'After I announced I was pregnant, they took me off a course. I kicked up a hell of a fuss and managed to get back on. There was a definite feeling among many people that I wouldn't be returning even though I said I would have to for financial reasons.'

Anne Y. is a solicitor in an Edinburgh practice which handles divorce. She was 38 when she became pregnant for the first time.

'You can imagine how pleased I was. It had taken a long time and the doctors were just about ready to kick-start my ovaries with hormones when it happened. Well, once it was confirmed, I saw no point in not telling my senior partner. I knew exactly where I stood legally. It was a big practice and there wouldn't have been any problem getting cover for me during maternity leave. My husband and I had no money problems, so we could afford a nanny and I was certain I would be coming back to work. I was also certain, though, that I wanted to take as much time off after the birth as possible. I would be 39 when the baby was born and I felt I'd waited a long time for it. I wanted as many of those precious early weeks as possible. And as an older woman, who had read almost every bit of advice ever written on the subject, I was worried about losing the baby and didn't want to risk anything before the birth either. Basically I wanted full maternity leave.

'So, pretty thrilled and clued up, I broke the news after the last client appointment of the day. Far from being pleased, my senior partner seemed to feel I'd been deceiving him all these years into thinking I was never going to have children. He actually said he had credited me with some dedication to the company. And this was before I'd told him I intended to take the full quota of leave. It was an icy, rather short meeting.

'A day or two later I gave him a formal letter spelling everything out. He remarked that the last solicitor who had been pregnant had given in her notice. I said I wouldn't be doing that and he said there were drawbacks to employing women. That was a real irony – one of the reasons I'd been taken on was because the expanding family law side of the business needed a woman. He never actually disputed any of my rights, but he began making life very difficult. Interesting cases were taken off my books, on the pretext that I might not be around to see them through. After a few weeks I was reduced to doing the stuff usually left to clerks and juniors – conveyancing and a few wills for real excitement. I remember thinking, "If he's like that now, what will he be like if I have to take time off because the baby's ill or something?" Then, he consulted every other solicitor about the design of new offices we were taking but never talked to me about it. It was a toss-up between deciding not to give in to him no matter what and deciding it wasn't worth the struggle. In the end I decided it wasn't worth the struggle. I resigned long before my maternity leave was due to start.'

Anne had 18 months at home – 'I loved all of it, even the grotty bits' – before joining another practice.

Don't be trapped into committing yourself to a return date as soon as you tell your boss you are pregnant. Say you'll be giving the details in writing when you've thought more about it. Remember, all you need give in writing BEFORE the birth is notice that you do intend to come back to work and that you will work until 11 weeks before the baby is due. When you do give a date, it'll be credit in the bank for the next pregnancy if you stick to it, so don't do it yet. And it's better to make it later, rather than earlier. You can always bring it forward.

If there are promotions in the air, say you'd like to be kept informed and to be considered for any positions that interest you. It all helps establish the picture of you as someone who intends to come back as a vital part of the company – which you are! Right now, you're very absorbed with the baby and with getting the best deal you can for your pregnancy, but there will come a time when you've returned to work and are ready for the next promotion. It's amazing how the mind clears when the baby is about six weeks old and you begin to feel normal again. You find your head rising above the cloud of cotton wool and baby powder it has been lost in for so long. Friends phone you and find you can talk, even if only briefly, about something other than your fascinating baby. You may even find yourself phoning colleagues for the latest office news. And caring about it, which is more than you did when they rang you earlier on, so it's worth bearing promotion in mind while you're still at work, and thinking ahead. In fact, with a family to think of, a promotion may be even more important to you than before.

Check you've gone through everything on your list, whether it's mental or written down. Say you'll be giving your boss a formal letter confirming you want to come back and ask for a letter from him confirming everything you have agreed.

Remember you're entitled to the legal minimum and you're worth any topping-up you can get! So don't be apologetic, don't act as if you're breaking bad news. Any sign of guilt will buy you the worst deal the company can get away with. Above all, be positive. Show that having a baby makes you happy, that you're confident everything will work out and that you're looking forward to starting again afterwards.

As the stories of Elaine Redding and all the others show, if your employer sacks you when he hears you're pregnant and you haven't worked the necessary minimum time, there's always the Sex Discrimination Act to fall back on. Dismissal for being pregnant is sexual discrimination and a tribunal may well award compensation. If you aren't protected by length of service and you are sacked for being pregnant, the Equal Opportunities Commission is legally obliged to help you.

The EOC can't take every case to a tribunal or a court, but it is the place to turn to if you run into problems with your employer because you're pregnant. If you are dismissed, the EOC is likely to send you Form SD74 (also available from your union, professional association or local Job Centre) which is in the form of a questionnaire. You will be asked to fill in your details and a summary of your complaint. You must sign and date the form, keep a copy and send the original by recorded delivery to your employer who will be asked to fill in the rest of the form to provide details from them about why you were dismissed, past records of other employees dismissed over the last two years and whether those who dismissed you had been given any equal opportunities training. The employer is not legally obliged to answer the questions, but as they will form part of your evidence, a tribunal may take refusal into account when considering your claim under the Sex Discrimination Act. To help you decide whether you have a claim, the EOC will send you a leaflet called *Pregnant – and lost your job?* The EOC will also tell you what to do next. It's advisable to get your professional association or union involved in your case.

Under the EC Pregnancy Directive, which must come into force before October 1994, employers will have to provide in writing their reasons for dismissing any pregnant employee. In Britain at any one time there are around 36,000 pregnant working professionals, 26,000 pregnant working managers and administrators and 120,000 pregnant secretarial/clerical workers.

While you're pregnant and at work, you may have worries about health and safety. The executive woman isn't likely to be heaving heavy weights around, but there are other concerns. Take your worries to your GP, the company nurse, your trade union. Working on personal computers seems to be the most frequent complaint among professional women and there's no cut and dried advice, although the most recent research does suggest that there is no harmful effect from working with PCs. I used mine throughout my pregnancy, but turned it off when I wasn't actually typing. A colleague refused to use hers from the beginning of her pregnancy and even turned the screen away from her. I was more concerned for my back and managed to get an adjustable footrest from the personnel department, which made life much more comfortable.

You have the right to paid time off for antenatal care during pregnancy, under the Employment Protection Act of 1980, whether you work full-time or part-time. Antenatal classes are a grey area. Few employers would give time off for them, but as they tend to be in the evenings anyway, few women are affected. At most antenatal centres, classes are one evening a week for six weeks.

The Act doesn't specify how much time you can have for care, but obviously covers regular clinic appointments and tests. Most GP practices and hospitals want to see you every four weeks until week 28, then every two weeks. Impress everyone by getting your appointments down in the office diary well ahead of time. Employers in practice seem not to raise difficulties about time off for checks.

4

The Elderly Primigravida: Medical matters

Only one person mentioned my age throughout my antenatal care. And that was me. I was 33 when I conceived, 34 when I gave birth. The medical people I saw – GP, midwife, nurse, radiologist, etc. – never expressed any worries on account of my age. When my midwife was arguing against a home birth, it was on the grounds of first-time, not late, motherhood. Oh, I occasionally dragged the subject up at the surgery, if I was uneasy, but it was obviously no consideration. I never felt this was neglect on their part, just reassuring confidence that all was well. Not that 34 is very old, but everyone else's absolute acceptance of it was something positive to weigh against vague feelings that with grey hairs multiplying I was rather ancient for this baby lark.

The average age at menopause now is 50 and, as we saw in the first chapter, more and more women are choosing to have first and second families late. So why this chapter? Partly to explore those vague feelings – they are based on facts and figures about maternal age after all – and partly to reassure you too. Age has its effect on fertility, conception, fetal abnormality and birth and this chapter will look at all of those. But this is not primarily a medical book and there'll be a list of where to go for further advice on any one of those subjects.

The executive woman is especially likely to leave motherhood late and so to be older than average when she starts to plan pregnancy. And the chances are that her partner will be older too. Fertility in both sexes is affected by age. It's also affected by alcohol in men and women and by smoking in men. Smoking in women has now been proved to increase the risk of miscarriage and leads to smallweight babies. Handicapped babies are also thought to be more likely. So start living healthily – both you and your partner – around three months before you start trying for a baby. The books on page 110 in the bibliography will help you. So will the Health Education Authority, whose address is in the back of the book. Check you've been vaccinated against rubella (German measles) and come off the Pill or coil three months beforehand as well. Use a barrier method for contraception until you both decide you are ready to conceive.

Let's look at the general fertility picture and then see how it is affected by age. As a post-Pill, career-oriented generation, we've spent so much time and effort over the years trying not to become pregnant that we rather tend to assume unprotected sex automatically equals baby. There's actually only a short time each month when conception is likely, which is why the average couple takes about four months before the woman conceives.

After six months of trying, four out of ten couples will still not have been lucky. On the bright side, in eight out of ten couples the women will have conceived within 12 months and this figure goes up to nine out of ten after two years. These are overall figures, of course. Couples in their thirties and forties are less fertile than teenagers or those in their twenties. By your late thirties, it takes an average of between six to nine months for a woman to conceive.

Fertility gradually declines in women from the age of 28 and the decline accelerates after 35. (Though there's something called the last fling of the ovaries around the age of 40 in which there's a sudden upsurge in fertility.) In your early twenties, you've got a 95 per cent chance of conceiving without any trouble. By your late thirties this is down to 75 per cent. Why? Well, if it's a long relationship, you simply may be having sex less often than you did when you first got together, but there are physiological reasons too.

Men are making sperm all the time whereas women are born with their lifetime's supply of eggs intact and ready to be released when the time is right. The older you are, the more likely your eggs are to have deteriorated and the more likely their release is to be erratic. On top of this, there's some evidence that the older womb is simply less good at hanging on to fertilised eggs which do successfully implant themselves. Injectable contraceptives and the Pill are also thought to delay conception.

If you keep trying at the right time every month and nothing happens, every period brings deep disappointment and, if it's a day or so late, another tenner or so spent on those wonderful home pregnancy tests you can get from the chemist. There are various ways of checking, by mucus and temperature, that you are having sex at your most fertile time every month. After all, eggs don't last much more than a day and sperm begin dying after about two or three days. One method frequently recommended is having sex four times over seven days, which guarantees live sperm are about all the time if an egg should pass by! If you've been through all that and there's still nothing happening, go to your GP. Most of them will consider tests after a year, though some may be more sympathetic towards older couples. Remember that one or two in ten couples have some problem in conceiving. Incidentally, you and your partner should both go: in at least a third of infertility cases, the problem lies with the man.

What are the problems? They're usually hormonal or to do with a failure to ovulate, a blockage or damage to the reproductive system. The first and third problems apply to men as well as women. Tests and treatment for infertility are available on the NHS, but there are waiting lists. The Family Planning Association estimates that private counselling, tests and treatment can cost up to £2,000. The FPA will answer very general queries but refers most women to either Issue or Child (see page 114).

You can join Issue, whose address is in the back of the book, for £30 for the first year, and £15 for subsequent years. It used to be called the National Association for the Childless, and has been going since 1976. Members receive factsheets and the latest articles on fertility tests and treatment, IVF clinics and donor insemination clinics; counselling and references to fertility experts. Members are also given the number of the Issue telephone support line, staffed by counsellors. Issue also offers support to those trying to adopt and those who are coping without children.

The charity Child is another resource. It has a medical adviser to whom you can write, as well as a 24-hour telephone line, a quarterly newsletter, factsheets and regional groups. See the back of the book for address details if you want to join. Factsheets on just about every aspect of infertility are available to non-members as well.

Tests for Women
- Daily temperature recording to monitor ovulation.
- An ultrasound scan will show visually, on a screen, whether the ovary has released an egg.
- Blood, urine and cervical mucus tests can be run to check hormonal levels and there's also an endometrial biopsy which

removes a small sample of womb lining to see how it's affected by changing hormone levels.

If these tests show all is clear, doctors may move on to check for a mechanical blockage or damage to the female system.

- Using laparoscopy, viewing with a minute telescope through a small cut below the navel, you'll be checked for scar tissue, fibroids and any oddity in the shape of the womb and the fallopian tubes.
- If there's nothing amiss with the external view of these organs, a hysterosalpingogram may be done. A special dye, visible on X-ray, is injected into the womb and tubes to show up any blockages and show the internal shape.
- If conception has been followed by miscarriage, the neck of the womb may be checked to see if it's strong enough to hold a fetus inside.

Tests for Men
- A sperm test examines the ejaculate and checks it for number of sperm, their shape and size and how well they move. And if your husband is reluctant to accept that the problem may lie with him, point out that it could be something as simple as wearing tight underpants which is causing the problem. Boxer shorts help breeding!
- Blood and urine tests can be done quite simply to check hormone levels. A testicular biopsy is a likely next step, which takes a small piece of tissue from each testis and checks on sperm production. Then there's the vasography, rather like the hysterosalpingogram for women, which checks for blockages in the vas deferens, the tubes on each side that carry sperm from the testicles.
- There's also a combined test to see how the sperm and the woman's mucus work together. There are cases of incompatibility. A few hours after sex, samples of cervical secretions are taken to see if the sperm are swimming freely and able to make headway towards a waiting egg.
- In some cases women are producing antibodies to their partner's sperm and killing them off. This one is easily treated with cortisone tablets and after that conception can be rapid.

Once you've found out what the problem is, there's the treatment. Blocked tubes can be opened up in both sexes – tricky surgery with variable success rates. Hormonal imbalances can be corrected by drugs, though some of these may carry a risk of multiple birth. Other options include artificial insemination, either by the husband or by a donor, and *in vitro* fertilisation, the so-called test-tube baby method, which means sperm meets egg in a special container and then the fertilised egg is placed in the womb.

There's a list of helpful reading on infertility in the bibliography at the back of the book. You can get more advice from Issue or Child.

Before you try to conceive, you may want to have a pre-conception check, which most GP surgeries do, on the NHS. You don't have to have one of these, but I rather enjoyed mine. Once you've decided you want to have a baby but you have not yet started trying, you can phone up your surgery and ask if they do them. It's little more than a chat with a few tests like weight and blood pressure thrown in. You're asked about your gynaecological history and your lifestyle. All quite painless. And it's a great opportunity to ask any questions about age and any special treatment your GP practice gives to older mothers. You may also wish to voice worries of problems which may have occurred to your own mother, e.g. miscarriages, difficult births, etc. For me, it was like putting down a definite marker. Another phase of my life was about to begin, nothing to do with my career, but everything to do with choice. I felt absurdly gratified to be told by the nurse I was 'a nice healthy lady'. In a way, it was like turning to pay attention to a side of me which had been ignored or left to bumble along in its own way for years, while other things took precedence. Not quite as good as being pregnant, but definitely a good thing to do.

Having said that, it was the first time I realised the medical profession's tendency to talk down to the rest of us. In my case, the culmination of this was going round the hospital and being told by a midwife there that the baby might 'do a poo' in the womb and paediatricians were referred to as baby-doctors. Women can do without the nursery language – especially Executive Mothers.

Even if you never bothered with an ovulation kit (a device which tells you when you're at your most fertile), the chances are you'll be tempted by one of the pregnancy tests you can buy from the chemist. They're so simple these days you don't have to bother with dipsticks and glass tubes. You just pee on the stick, which will produce a blue line, or maybe a pink dot, depending on the make you've chosen, if you're pregnant, and will stay blank if you're not.

The instructions include a warning not to splash the windows, which I thought was pretty unlikely until I realised they didn't mean the bathroom windows, but the indicator windows. They can give you a result the day your period is due, albeit a very faint result, so if you're anything like I was, you'll be there on the day, holding a stick up to the light, trying desperately to see dots or lines. Not convinced by what I saw, I would try another one a couple of days later, which, at about a tenner for two sticks, is a pretty expensive obsession. They're very accurate and much quicker than taking a specimen to your doctor and waiting until the result comes back from the hospital. My husband claimed he couldn't really see much of a dot and was only truly convinced by a much darker result a few days later, by which time we were on holiday in a French gîte, a rotten time and place to give up alcohol, even for the best of reasons. It wasn't just wishful thinking on my part: I knew that if I hadn't wanted to be pregnant, that almost invisible shade of pink would have sent me into a frenzy of worry.

You've decided to have your baby, you've done what you can to prepare yourself and now you've had your pregnancy confirmed. The one thing which crosses every mother's mind now is: 'Will the baby be all right?' And older mothers are probably more concerned than most about abnormalities, which they fear may be age-related. Down's syndrome, or mongolism, is the big worry of a woman having children later. At the age of 20, the risk is around one in 2,000. By the age of 50, it's one in ten. And for those women married to older men, it's worth remembering that there's some evidence that paternal age makes Down's more likely over 55.

Maternal Age	Risk	Maternal Age	Risk
20	1:1923	41	1:85
30	1:885	42	1:70
35	1:365	43	1:50
36	1:290	45	1:32
37	1:225	46	1:25
38	1:180	47	1:20
39	1:140	48	1:15
40	1:109	49	1:12

So the risk is there, but the figures hide another story. Today, babies with Down's syndrome are more likely to be born to younger women because older women tend to have the tests we'll be looking at later in the chapter. Between the ages of 35 and 39 the risk of a baby with any sort of chromosomal disorder, including Down's, has been calculated at one in 70. Spina bifida, an exposure of the spinal column, and other malformations of the central nervous system, are thought not to be age-related. If spina bifida has occurred in your family, or if you have already had a child with spina bifida, your baby is more likely to be affected, ten times more likely, according to some research. Spina bifida is still something of a mystery, but is thought to be linked to folic acid and vitamin deficiency.

While we're looking at the drawbacks of getting pregnant later in life, let's include the effect on the health of the mother – the elderly primigravida. You are more likely to get various ailments, but remember that just the fact that you're reading this book makes it less likely that you belong to the real high-risk group of socially deprived mothers, who of course affect statistics.

Here's the doom list of what you're more likely to suffer because you're older:

> higher chance of miscarriage and morning sickness in the first three months
> higher blood pressure with the possibility of pre-eclampsia
> slightly higher possibility of diabetes
> placenta praevia, when the placenta is over the entrance to the womb and can cause haemorrhage
> premature onset of labour in the first pregnancy

Read *Birth Over Thirty* by Sheila Kitzinger, for a detailed run-down.

While you're drawing breath and wondering whether you'll survive the experience, remember that if you're well-nourished and healthy and in your late thirties, you're still a better medical bet than a young woman who lives on chips, smokes and generally doesn't look after herself.

Five per cent of women over 35 are likely to haemorrhage because of placenta praevia or other reasons, compared to three per cent of women ten years younger. The risk of high blood pressure goes up by 50 per cent in the mid to late thirties. If it's combined with oedema or fluid retention, there's a possibility of pre-eclampsia or, logically enough, eclampsia, a convulsive condition which can be life-threatening to the mother. Very high blood pressure can affect the baby too, by preventing the placenta from working properly. But again, 'lifestyle' factors come into play.

If you are getting proper antenatal care and keeping your clinic appointments, a check will be kept on all these things with blood tests, urine tests and blood pressure readings. Ultrasound scans pick up, among other things, placenta praevia. For reassurance, ask the questions. There's no point in worrying unnecessarily – it sends your blood pressure up. At one of my early clinics I had a high blood pressure reading which the doctor said was borderline for treatment. She would check it next time. She did and after that it crept steadily downwards. Fluke readings are all too likely if you've rushed to your appointment from work, driven to the surgery through traffic or done anything to make you hot and bothered.

Antenatal care, whether it's at a hospital or at your local GP surgery, can seem like a succession of urine samples and weight-checks. But there are also special tests to check for abnormalities.

Amniocentesis
Amniocentesis detects Down's syndrome as well as spina bifida. In the amniocentesis, at about 16 weeks, amniotic fluid is drawn off into a needle passed through the womb wall. It's done in conjunction with a scan, to avoid puncturing the baby. A culture of cells is grown so the chromosomes can be examined. This takes time and the result rarely comes through for another two or three weeks. The way in which the test is offered and the age at which it is offered varies from centre to centre. The test itself can cause miscarriage – there's about a one in 100 chance – so it makes sense to offer it only to mothers at risk because of age or family history. At some clinics this means 35 and over; others wait until 37. If you're not in a high-risk group, but you still want it done, either ask for it or have it done privately. It's worth checking your GP practice for their attitude towards tests and terminations – you may find you're in 'born-again' hands!

Triple test
These days the definitive amniocentesis is usually preceded by the so-called triple test – a blood test which measures the level of alphafetoprotein, lower in Down's syndrome, higher in spina bifida. For this to be effective, an ultrasound scan is given to assess exactly how pregnant you are, and so how much alphafetoprotein

should be in the blood at this stage. A high reading can be an indicator of a neural tube defect such as spina bifida. The drawback to the test is that it is just that: an indicator, which doesn't mean there's necessarily anything wrong with the baby you're carrying. If it's a raised reading, you'll be offered an amniocentesis: a difficult choice for a woman not yet in the higher age bracket, because of the miscarriage risk. Talk to the doctor, talk to the consultant, make sure you and your partner are satisfied that you've been given the information to make an informed choice. At 33, once I'd had an ultrasound scan at 14 weeks and seen what was definitely a mini-baby bobbing about, I decided against the triple test. But everyone is different.

Ultrasound scans are diagnostic and not for finding out the sex of your baby, though some radiographers will tell you. How many scans you have will depend on your antenatal centre, but most women have one at around 18 weeks, as well as the pre-triple test scan. A scan shows how pregnant you are, how the baby is lying and how active it is and can show any spinal defects. If the baby is lying awkwardly or if the placenta is low-lying, you will probably have several scans. As far as we know, they are harmless.

An equally accurate alternative to amniocentesis is chorionic villus sampling, which takes placental tissue via a needle inserted through the cervix, using ultrasound. The big advantage is that it can be done between eight and ten weeks, which makes any termination far less traumatic, but it carries a slightly higher miscarriage risk than amniocentesis. And it's not available everywhere because of cost. A woman with a family history may well want to demand the test because of the early result. If it isn't available in your area, insist on a referral elsewhere.

Read *Down Syndrome: the Facts*, by Mark Selikowitz (Oxford Paperbacks) for a very good description of both tests and an examination of what the syndrome is, its different degrees and life with a Down's child.

The chorionic villus sampling, like the amniocentesis, is performed at an outpatients' clinic. The earliest possible time it can be done is six weeks after the date of your last period. Small finger-like pieces of tissues are sucked up to be grown in the laboratory. The chromosomes are stained and examined. Results are available in two days, but most labs like to do a more detailed examination which takes around two weeks. The miscarriage risk with CV at nine weeks is between three and four in a hundred. Neither test can tell you the degree of abnormality.

If the tests prove positive, you will be offered an abortion. You should also be offered counselling to help you with your decision. If not, ask for it or contact the Down's Syndrome Association, for helpful advice (see Useful Addresses on page 114). If you decide to go ahead with an abortion it will be done in hospital and induced by a drip which starts the womb contracting so it expels its contents.

As an older woman, used to responsibility and decision-making at work, you're well-placed to cope with the medical system and not to become just a number. You're more likely to be in the same social group and earning bracket as your doctor. You'd talk to each other as equals at the dinner table: why not in the surgery? The chances are you will read books and ask questions about your antenatal care and make your own decisions on the medical advice you're given. It's the same with deciding where you would like to have your baby, whether it's at home or in hospital. Don't make a blind choice: talk to the doctor, the midwife and other recent mothers. Find out what's available in your area. You may prefer the idea of delivery in a birthing pool: see if it's on offer. These days, pain relief is available underwater in some hospitals. Some women, having found a willing midwife, hire a birthing pool for a home birth and even use it for a few days afterwards for family baths, baby and all.

Even if you think you've made up your mind, phone the maternity hospital to find out when they do tours for expectant couples. It's often at the weekend. You and your partner can go along and be shown the labour rooms and wards and even some of the methods of pain relief. I went along worried that a hospital birth might still mean lying down in bed covered in monitors and was pleasantly surprised to be shown labour rooms complete with bean bags, cassette players and rocking chairs. One room, sponsored by Marks and Spencer, even had pretty wallpaper and curtains. And we were shown the gas and air cylinders and the so-called TENS machine, which scrambles the pain signals during labour. It all helped to take the fear out of the technology. It gave me a picture in my head of where I was having my baby. Another couple being shown round at the same time had almost decided in favour of a home birth but were just checking the options. In other words, it's worth taking every opportunity of gathering information before you choose where to have your baby.

Again, older mothers are more likely to have certain problems during labour, and again it's all too easy to exaggerate them, but that's no reason to ignore them. Some sources say a longer labour is likely. Prolonged or difficult labour can end in a forceps delivery, though in some hospitals these days the more European ventouse or vacuum extractor is used – rather more comfortable for the mother and apparently as safe for the baby.

Certainly older women tend to have more caesarian sections and forceps deliveries. Around 30 per cent of first-time mothers over 35 have caesarian sections. Caesarian section is a controversial business in the maternity world, so it's worth discussing it with your consultant or GP beforehand so you're well-informed if it should become an option for you. Reasons for a caesarian being especially likely in older mothers include pre-eclampsia and placenta praevia.

Once you're over 35, induction of labour is more likely, because the chances of a sudden last-minute rise in blood pressure are higher. Hospitals generally though are no longer induction-mad as they were a few years ago, because the widespread use of ultrasound scans means a much more precise idea of when the baby is really due. My daughter was born three weeks after the due date, by both my calculations and two scans at 14 and 19 weeks. When I was ten days late, I went to hospital for a scan and fetal monitor, which showed all was well. Then I had a couple more routine appointments for monitoring before I was booked in for an induction. My baby was born the night before.

A final word. More and more hospitals these days are getting used to mothers turning up with a birth plan. I thought the whole idea sounded rather too trendy, but when we visited the hospital a few days before the baby was due, the midwives were surprisingly positive about it. With an increasing number of older, more confident first-time mothers, they've probably had to get used to it. It smooths continuity of care if one midwife's shift ends and another comes on duty part way through labour: she can pass your plan on to the next one. It's a help to the midwives to know, for example, whether you mind having student medics in the labour room, how you feel about episiotomy, whether you'd like to deliver the placenta naturally or, as is usual, with the help of a drug to speed it up. Discuss with your partner what sort of birth you'd like and make a simple plan on one side of a sheet of paper. Keep it short, covering his role, pain relief and whether you'd like to be in bed or upright.

Remember you can change your mind about anything. If you

opt for a birth without pain relief, you can still demand everything they've got if the pangs are too much. Putting pen to paper doesn't commit you to anything, especially not to being brave if you no longer feel it. My own birth plan kept being pushed further and further back in my case notes as midwife succeeded midwife. Not that I minded.

I'd said, as I would say again, that I'd like as natural a birth as possible, with as little pain relief as I could get by with, maybe using the TENS machine from the beginning of my labour and gas and air towards the end. In the early part of my time in hospital, all went as we'd hoped: we had Vivaldi on the labour room cassette player and I was occasionally changing position to keep comfortable on a wonderfully huge bean bag. But, in the event, our daughter was born 42 hours after the first contraction. Simple exhaustion took over by midday on the second day and I needed an epidural, which was gratefully received, as well as Syntocinon to speed up the later contractions. Remembering my birth plan, I was rueful, but very pleased I had added the rider that I might not be as brave as I thought and might change my mind.

5

Time Out:
Going forth to multiply

Your maternity leave may begin with a bunch of flowers from colleagues, with a farewell drink or with just a quiet exit from the office, but however it starts, it will almost certainly be the longest break you've ever had from work. And it's a shock. For years, work has come first and, for those of us who have inevitably defined ourselves by the job we do, it can be rather unnerving to become a non-person to The Office for several months. Older women considering how much of a break they want tend to under-estimate how it will feel. Convinced of our own indispensability at work, and being fairly clueless about what life after baby will bring, we often try to work on as late as possible in the pregnancy and aim to be back as soon as possible after the birth.

Susie J., a university geography lecturer, said:

'I think this is one area where career women miss out. I've heard other women say how much they enjoyed being pregnant, but I can't say I ever felt that. I was perfectly well most of the time and it was okay, but I did feel I was fighting it, that I was working in spite of being pregnant, making life go on as normal when actually I hadn't been pregnant before and it was anything but normal.

'There was no clear beginning to my maternity leave, because I kept doing some work with students until the last minute, so I never really relaxed into being pregnant. I can't say that I ever thought much beyond the birth, either, never thought how life was likely to be. I remember sitting in a tiny Italian restaurant with my husband a few weeks before the baby was due. There was one window table for four and I said to him it would be a nice table to reserve for when his parents came to stay and see the baby. He chuckled and said: "Fine, where's the baby going to be?'' I think if I'd had time at home to adjust, the whole thing would have seemed more real.'

Others take the view that, having put work first for so long, it's time to do this next job – having a baby – with equal dedication and decide to take the maximum maternity leave. Chapter 3 outlines the different arrangements and there are as many as there are career women. We looked at the different rights to pay and leave but you may want to tailor-make your own leave within those rights.

There's no reason why you should seal yourself off from a job which is important to you, either before or after the birth. In practice few career women do, especially those who plan to go on and up after the baby. I chose to do the most important single part of my job – a Wednesday page in the *Daily Express* – throughout my maternity leave for several reasons. I love it; it could be done easily from home; and in the uncertain world of newspapers I could scarcely hope that no rival would fill the breach over several months. I sent one column, thanks to the magic of laptop computers and modems, at 2 a.m. when the first birth pangs came on. And, because our daughter was born conveniently on a Wednesday, I had somehow scraped up enough energy to write another column by the next deadline.

But before then, a week or so into my maternity leave, a call came from the office to say an interview had been planned at Number 10 with Norma Major, the Prime Minister's wife, just days before the expected announcement of the 1992 General Election. The *Express* didn't want me to feel I HAD to agree to do it. I did agree, of course. It was a one-off too good to miss and I felt quite fit enough to do it. Other women are rather more extreme, choosing to work in the office almost until their due dates, fitting in medical appointments and antenatal classes as best they can. It really depends on how you feel late in your pregnancy and what kind of work you do. Only you will know what you can manage.

In a survey by the Maternity Alliance, an astonishing 31 per cent of women had been asked to do some work while on maternity leave. You've every right to say no, of course, but you may feel it's worth doing some work, so long as it is something reasonable and/or to your benefit. It's a difficult balancing act, because most career women who want to return to work after maternity leave will probably want to keep in touch with what's going on. And many employers seem to find it hard to distinguish between someone who wants office memos, details of courses and copies of the trade press sending to her while she's pregnant and someone who actually wants to or doesn't mind working. Legally, it's cut and dried: on maternity leave you don't have to do any work at all. In practice it's anything but, so don't be taken by surprise. Know what you think. It's awful to hear yourself saying yes when you're really feeling no.

Nearly all the career women I have talked to opted not to take the full 11 weeks maternity leave before the birth, so that they would have extra weeks with the baby afterwards. Of course, if you're not well enough to work, or to travel a long distance to work, your doctor will sign you off without loss of leave. Most women work until about six weeks before their due date, and feel a huge sigh of relief as the office door closes behind them, knowing it will be months before they have to go into work again. Many women have used a considerable amount of determination to keep going very late into the pregnancy and they often report flopping completely for the first week or so of maternity leave.

Before that door closes, some women, although they needn't do so, choose to tell their employer they will be back at their desks by a particular date – usually early. You may feel this earns you brownie points, but if you haven't had a baby before it's probably unwise to commit yourself to a return date, because you don't know how you're going to feel. The chances are that you will want to spend longer than you imagine with your baby, especially if you are breastfeeding. And remember, if the baby is late you will have less time to spend with her before going back to work, unless you have a remarkably understanding employer. Maternity leave is calculated in advance, by the due date.

And while you're thinking of when to take what leave, bear in mind that you may, as I did (I sometimes feel this book is developing into a cautionary tale), go briefly batty in the days after the birth. In my case, sleeping in the hospital had been almost impossible, and the tiredness coupled with the usual postnatal hormone riot led to a ghastly 'I can't cope' state which lasted two or three days. There was one day when I kept walking past the slice of toast my husband had made me for breakfast, meaning to eat it, but never having the time because there was always something which had to be done first! I was very glad not to have committed myself to going back early. It meant that by the time I turned up in the office to discuss things with my editor and show off the baby we both looked pretty fit and well, in spite of the broken nights. And, the bonus of breastfeeding, I was half a stone lighter than before I was pregnant!

But we haven't got to that stage yet. Antenatal classes usually begin – if you decide you want them – in the evenings while still going into work, but it's really only when maternity leave begins that you start discovering a world outside work. My own antenatal classes, run at a local clinic, didn't last long because I was so disappointed with them. It took the midwife and health visitor in charge of the sessions so long to impart so little information I found I was better off reading a few books.

If you decide you want to go to classes, start phoning round long before your maternity leave to find out when they begin and how many weeks they last. A course run by the National Childbirth Trust which I enquired about lasted nine weeks and was well underway before I'd even thought about it. I couldn't fit the classes in before my due date. NCT classes tend to be smaller than NHS classes, because they're usually held in the teacher's home – another reason for thinking and booking ahead. The NHS classes of course are taken by people with medical qualifications and are often in hospitals, day centres or local clinics. If you're keen on an intervention-free labour or a home birth, the Active Birth Centre (see page 114) may be able to put you in touch with a regular class in your area.

The local branch of the National Childbirth Trust, whether or not you go to the antenatal classes, may well be worth joining. It costs £15 to join and between £30 and £70 for antenatal classes, depending on the branch. If work has been your social life as well, it's very strange to find yourself out on a limb, or to discover that you and your colleagues suddenly have very different ideas of what is a conversational topic of burning interest. Remember how your eyes used to glaze over when a pregnant colleague would confide this urgent problem over a quiet lunch: whether to go for terries or disposables, a traditional pram or a three-in-one combination job? Well, only the voice has changed. It's yours now.

Organisations like the NCT can provide friends as well as advice. There are social events where pregnant women and new mothers can mix and there are talks and breastfeeding counselling on offer too. Most branches hold nearly new sales of baby equipment and have a lending library. It could be a few pounds well spent. You may even, if you're suffering withdrawal from management, find a committee to serve on or a summer strawberry tea to organise. Some career women find they can't bear the coffee-morning world: others take to it hugely. As a commuter, I started my maternity leave with the realisation that my friends were scattered inaccessibly all over the country and that for several years I'd used the town where I lived simply as a railway station. I was looking forward to making new friends. It's worth remembering that other career women have babies too: you won't be the only one.

And, surprise, surprise, you may discover less high-powered women as friends too. As one woman, now 48, put it: 'This was the first time in my life I'd mixed on an equal footing with women who hadn't all followed my path of university, professional training and career. It taught me that I could have friendships with all sorts of women.'

Once you are on maternity leave, you'll have time to think about the birth, read the books, and talk to other women and midwives about it and make a choice. You may decide you want an active birth or even a water birth. Now's the time to read all about it and get going on the old exercise routines, if that's what you want. It's also the time to decide on your birth plan, that piece of paper you take with you to the hospital.

And this is the last time – sobering thought – that you and your partner will be alone for years, so it's worth trying to make it a specially intimate time, even if your head is full of baby things. If you feel confident enough, you could even have a fairly easy-going holiday, checking first with your doctor. Anne, the solicitor who resigned from her company over her pregnancy, found she suddenly had lots of precious time before the birth.

'My husband had been reading all the men chapters in my pregnancy books and was prepared to be a hero throughout – you know: painting windowsills, going without sex and being understanding when I cried buckets. He had New Man practically written on his forehead. So it was rather wonderful to be able to shrug off work, stop being superwoman and book us a two-week holiday in Florence, just when he was preparing for martyrdom.

'The doctor wrote me a note for the airline – I was 28 weeks pregnant. It was the sort of holiday it would be really daunting to go on with children. We had a blissful time in churches, galleries and restaurants and I know we'll both remember it for ever. It was a way of taking advantage of a turn of events I hadn't expected – leaving my job. And it was a chance to devote myself entirely to Jim before the baby filled my head. A lovely, lovely time.'

Anne also found she had lots of time after the holiday to sort things out at home, getting ready for the baby and rather enthusiastically sampling three different kinds of antenatal class.

'It also gave me time to talk to Jim's daughter from his first marriage about the baby. She was 15 and I'd left actually breaking the news of the pregnancy entirely up to him. I found she appreciated being in on all the girly things, like choosing a carrycot. And she loved putting her hand on my stomach and feeling the baby move. We redecorated the room she sleeps in when she comes to stay, so she realised she was part of this new phase too. I couldn't believe it when she started talking about babysitting. Acceptance was the most I'd hoped for, but she looked forward to the baby with absolute relish. If I'd been working up to the last minute. I'd have let things like that go and had much less patience.'

I found that in the weeks before the birth, even though I was writing a regular column, working on this book, and doing quite a bit of extra sleeping, I still had time and even energy (thank God for iron tablets) to indulge two ambitions: reading *Middlemarch* and teaching myself the basics of Italian. Will I ever have such spare time again?

You should also use this time to sort out childcare for when you go back to work, or at least to investigate it. It may seem a long way off now, but once the baby has arrived, the time will go quickly. See chapters 7 and 8!

This is definitely a time you'll be buying things and it's best to be cautious. It's a long time since your own mother had children, so you get less up-to-date advice from that quarter on what you should buy than younger first-time mothers do. And your mother will have long since given up on you as a source of grandchildren and either handed baby things to someone more productive or decided she needed the space in the attic for something else. The chances are that you just haven't been moving in baby circles and don't have much of an idea. This is a whole new world.

The first time I stood in Mothercare and thought, 'Should all this be mine?' I was lost and so alarmed that I came out with nothing, putting off what now seemed like the evil day. Whatever decisions you've been used to taking in your working life, you can feel utterly bewildered when faced with choosing the sort of baby bath you want, let alone whether to go for a steam steriliser or a tank. And yes, there is a forest of possibilities between the Mary Poppins full-scale pram and the flimsy buggy with deckchair stripes. When you do go shopping, don't be bullied into buying anything and don't overdo it. It's tempting to get everything in one big sweep, feeling that you've got the money, you've waited a long time for it all and anyhow that must be the most efficient way of doing it. The trouble is, it's also the most efficient way of spending what you may not need to spend.

The shops will still be open after your baby is born and, as an Executive Mother, you'll find yourself quite mobile enough to get out and about with your baby. One of the most wonderful discoveries is that motion makes babies go to sleep, whether they're in a pram, a sling or a car seat. As long as they're not ravenous, of course. I nervously packed my four-week-old daughter into the car for our first solo shopping trip and then, in the multi-storey car park, stowed her in her carrier on my chest. I couldn't believe it when she slept round Marks and Spencer, a building society, a jewellery shop and Mothercare. It was like being given my driving licence all over again. So I wasn't housebound, after all!

I remember, four weeks before my due date, seeing the nursery of another woman whose baby was due ten days after mine. It seemed there was nothing she hadn't thought of, then bought. There was drawer after drawer of baby clothes, nearly all in the first size – more than any baby could hope to get through before outgrowing them. The pushchair had every accessory you could think of, including matching parasol. There was an activity mat which would have to be stored for months and a teddy bear the size of a one-year-old. Actually, in spite of her firm conviction that she was having a dark-haired boy, she had a ginger girl, so either a lot of blue things were returned to the shops or her little girl grew up splendidly unhampered by gender role-play.

Friends and relatives can be reluctant to come forward with offers of hand-me-downs because they fear they may offend, especially if they know you should have no trouble affording new things. But, unless you're determined to have everything new, decent hand-me-downs can save buying things the baby will be growing out of in a few weeks. Our baby was so long, her sleepsuits were soon pushed to the back of a drawer because she couldn't stretch her legs out in them.

Basically, as long as you have the necessary minimum of clothes and the maximum amount of cotton wool, clothes gaps can be filled in later. But, of course you will want to buy some things. Scratching your head for where baby things come from, it's hard to come up with anything but the chain stores if you've never had to do more than buy a Peter Rabbit mug for a cousin's baby. But there are the department stores and the small independent shops as well. The more you look first, the better idea you will form and the less likely you are to be landed with something you later find you don't want. Things change in the babyworld just as in any other consumer field. Go looking for frilly matinée jackets and bootees and the chances are you'll find nothing but a sea of all-in-one suits. Car travel has had its (expensive) effect on carrying baby around as well, but a baby seat is your passport to freedom, so it's best bought before the birth. It's useful to learn how it works beforehand as well.

You will find you need an assistant to explain everything to you and your partner, or whoever else is with you as moral support to make sure that if you'd rather go away and think first, you go away and think. A pram or pushchair/carrycot combination can set you back a few hundred pounds, after all. Be wary of the assistant who has spotted an Executive Mother-to-be.

When I was looking at all the carrycot accessories, I came across a sort of padded sleeping-bag affair labelled Cosytoes, which the assistant assured me was 'absolutely vital in cold weather'. I looked rather sceptical and she added: 'Well, unless you just put extra blankets round the baby.' An amazing number of things can be 'absolutely vital' if you believe what you're told by the people trying to sell them to you. So many things, it makes you wonder how your own mother could have brought you up successfully without them. Others, of course, are unnecessary but labour- or time-saving and probably worth the money.

Sceptical though I was about the Cosytoes, the same assistant did succeed in selling me a pack of expensive muslin squares. They're apparently to do with terry nappies, but I was using disposables and never worked out what I could do with them. They sit in a drawer waiting until I desperately need to strain fruit to make crab-apple jelly or something similar.

The most frightening thing I had to buy was a breast pump, which I kept looking at in Boots over several weeks before I actually bought it. Somehow this device seemed to epitomise the fact that I was about to be taken over by something primitive, uncontrollable and distinctly messy, which actually sounds like a perfect description of a baby as well as breastfeeding. If you intend to breastfeed, you may sometimes want to express your own milk. It means that you can clear off for a while, either to work or just for a sanity-preserving break, while someone else bottle-feeds the baby with your milk.

Apart from your own hands, there are several different types of pump on the market, both hand- and battery-operated, and it's best to ask your midwife's advice on what to buy. It's also advisable to try it for fit. Just along the shelf from the pump were the breast pads, further evidence of chaos to come for the mother who wants to combine breastfeeding with work. 'There's no worse feeling than thinking of your baby around feeding time and suddenly knowing the milk is coming through your shirt front and any minute now is likely to splash on your keyboard,' a colleague of mine, back from having the second of her babies, once said. 'You're not dealing with anything rational.' Hence the breast pads with waterproof backing, which if you're at home can probably be substituted with cotton-wool pads or folded handkerchiefs, become a boon when you're going out or going to work. A thought can trigger a leak. And patterned tops are the best disguise of wet patches.

Some women find that when they're not buying during their maternity leave, they're showing signs of domesticity which they once might have found worrying. A Fleet Street colleague of mine, eight months pregnant, was discovered by her husband, astride the bath painting the walls. He persuaded her to come down, only to find her some hours later wedged between the loo, the floor and the walls, trying to paint behind the cistern. Even if you have domestic help, there's an urge to do something in the house yourself. I found myself plotting how I might clean the windows and wax the pine dresser without being spotted by my husband who would have thought I was going barmy. I was supposed to be working on this book in the study and kept sneaking time off to go and clear out a drawer or something like that. The nesting instinct can make home-birds out of the most career-minded of women.

The second stage of maternity leave of course is after the birth and this is when your perspective on life, work and the world in general tends to alter, even if you don't go batty for a few days. Some women, naturally, are more resilient than others. Margaret

Thatcher continued with her legal studies after her twins were born and took her final bar exams when they were only four months old. 'We had help with the children. We lived in London. And eventually by sheer effort of will and driving myself and staying up very late at night I managed to take my finals. It was a colossal effort of will,' she told radio presenter Pete Murray in 1982. The following year she was called to the bar.

Once the baby is born, the previous few weeks can appear oddly dreamlike. You can't believe how little you guessed how much life was going to change. You bought all the clothes and the baby equipment. You read all the books. You probably, if you were more conscientious than I was, did all the exercises too. But somehow, either the books all stopped with the descriptions of the birth, or you simply never read on.

How could you have embarked on looking after this speechless, dependent little thing with so little preparation? I could have delivered a lecture on the varieties of pain relief available during labour, but I'd done nothing towards learning about babies. (By the way, the NCT runs a helpline for new mothers and a counselling service if you're having trouble breastfeeding.) What I would do after coming home from the hospital was all very vague to me – on the day itself I couldn't believe they let me go off, in charge of a baby, without L-plates. All my thoughts beforehand were concentrated on the actual birth. In fact, I wondered afterwards if I would have been less worried about that trauma if I'd spent more energy on getting used to the idea of having a baby in the house. So one other thing you could do in the weeks before the birth is to find out about babycare classes, through the NCT or other groups like the La Leche League and the Active Birth Group. Or go along to the coffee mornings and make friends with mothers and ask if you can visit a local nursery.

Your life, even this vastly altered new life, is not your own immediately the pair of you are discharged from hospital. A community midwife will visit you every day for ten days. After that, a health visitor will visit you once a week. And you may want to go along to a weekly clinic to have your baby weighed. At first, it is amazingly difficult to get anything done during the day apart from looking after the baby. The list of things to be done just appears to get longer and longer and the daily challenge is getting the baby looking decent and yourself looking and sounding like someone fit to be in charge of an infant, before the midwife comes.

The fact is, of course, that they're used to seeing all sorts of domestic chaos and yours is unlikely to be the worst.

You'll be deluged with advice from more experienced mothers. It's amazing how fashions in babycare change. If you're demand-feeding, you'll be told the virtues of four-hourly discipline by your elders. If you're determined to go with the broken nights until baby finds her own pattern, you'll be urged to give her baby rice or cereal to make her sleep through. Keeping her too hot, too cold; bathing her daily or weekly; putting her down for a regular nap or waiting until she seems tired: all these things and many more will beat around your eardrums with every visit or phone call.

But, of course, you may also want to seek, as I did, not so much advice, as other mothers' experiences. It's very comforting to realise that babies, mothers and marriages survive your trials and worse. I was forever asking other women questions, whether they were friends or simply people I came across at the clinic or in the supermarket queue. You discover motherhood is a whole new area of interest. After years of avoiding the topic, finding it dull or at least nothing to do with me, I found it underrated and fascinating.

Caring for your baby and enjoying her go without saying during this period, but eventually you also begin to think about your return to work. At first, when successful grooming is finding a clean, doubtless unironed, T-shirt every morning, it's hard to believe you ever will. After a few weeks, you will begin to have an idea of how you feel about your new life, whether you want work to be just as it was, or adapted in some way to suit your new status as mother. The next few chapters should help.

6

Going Back to Work: As you were or all change?

It sounds like a joke, but some women do return to work after their maternity leave and find their desk has gone. Or it has been given to somebody else and the things they left in their drawers – internal phone directories, train timetables, maps of the London underground – have either disappeared or been crammed into one drawer and the others filled with someone else's belongings. You could face this and more: the departmental secretary has changed and the new one doesn't know who you are; you're not on the phone list; you're not receiving internal mail; in spite of your arrangements, no one has bothered to deal with what mail you have received because you haven't been around to chase things up; there will possibly be new people there who will treat you as the latest arrival, especially if you have to ask them where the coffee machine has been relocated.

All this is not the confidence booster you need when you return to work that first morning, wondering whether motherhood has robbed you of your brain cells and whether the childminder really understood that the baby wasn't to be given artificially sweetened drinks. You may well be wondering whether you can still do your job, which of course you can, but you'll also be wondering whether your colleagues think you can. Women without children are often guilty of thinking that women with children think of nothing else. And there are still some men who think women with children should think of nothing else. One Executive Mother said:

'Not only had my desk gone, but it was explained to me that the company couldn't possibly offend the man occupying it by moving him. I objected quite strongly at first, but then I caved in. Somewhere at the back of my mind I still thought I owed the company, my boss and colleagues, something for maternity leave. Part of me felt I'd worked a buckshee holiday. A desk was found, though not in such a nice position.'

The way to avoid the whole ghastly scenario is to take charge of it. Just deciding to do that will make you feel more businesslike. And do it before it really gets under way. Would you sit down to feed your baby without having tissues handy? Well, don't go back to work without taking precautions against messiness either.

Instead of treating back-to-work day like the beginning of a new term at school and just turning up for it, put in a non-working visit a week or two beforehand, letting the people who matter know that you're coming in. There's no need to stay a long time: you don't want to feel like a spare part. If you want to show the baby off to your colleagues, don't do it on this visit. Now's the time to think professional, not parent. So fix the baby up with feeds and a minder and then forget her. And if you're breastfeeding, don't forget the pads. You want to present a businesslike front, not a milky one.

Phone your boss's secretary and fix a time to see him, not too early in the day, so you can see other people in the office first and catch up on things. That way, if there's anything really serious you haven't been able to solve, like that missing desk for instance, you can take it up with him. It's well worth having a chat, without overdoing the babytalk, of course, to re-establish yourself as part of his team.

Ask lots of questions, reassure him you've got the childcare sorted out and let him see you're keen to be back. Rack your brains and ask him what happened to such and such a project, what new things are in the pipeline, what happened at the latest think-tank. Treat it in the same spirit as an interview for a new job: sell yourself!

It will give him a chance to think of you afresh, how you might be used and what opportunities he can offer you. If the first time he sees you is 9 a.m. on the day you're due back, he'll be less likely to do that. He'll just think you've resumed the status quo, more because you have to than out of any real enthusiasm for the job.

But before that interview go on your tour. If you have an immediate superior, talk to her or him first and find out what's been going on and whether there have been any changes. Ask who's been promoted. Smile at whoever is sitting in your desk and gently remind her of the date you'll be sitting there again.

Take something in – a clearly labelled diary or address book – and install it in your top drawer. Check your in-tray for mail. Make a phone call from your extension. Enough to make her realise she's a tenant, not an owner-occupier.

Of course, it's rather more serious if your desk has actually gone. Take steps to make sure one is made available and will be there on the day you return to work, complete with phone, trays, word processor, whatever you work with. It's worth being firm. It really is a confidence shatterer to walk in and find there's nowhere to put your briefcase.

Talk to the secretarial staff, make sure you have the supplies you need and that the switchboard knows when you'll be back at your desk to take calls. If you've lost your business cards in the turmoil of the last few months, get the stationery department to do new ones. If there's an automatic ID card to get you into the building and you've lost it, arrange for another one. You don't want to turn up on your first day back labelled 'visitor'. It all helps to make you feel your professional self again.

If necessary, organise a mini mailshot round your clients or people you deal with regularly letting them know you're back in business. Arrange to take someone out to lunch. Fill in a few gaps in that diary. If there's any new equipment about that you're going to need to use, fix yourself a training session. Make sure the personnel department knows you're back. Go very easy on the baby snapshots. It's yourself as working professional, not as mother, whom you're trying to re-establish in your own eyes and everyone else's.

Of course, this is assuming you want to go back to work. If you're reading this book, the chances are that you do. Professional women are very likely to go back to work, and for more reasons than merely the money: the reasons which made them choose their career and advance so far in it.

The Policy Studies Institute interviewed 1,400 women for its 1991 report, *Maternity Rights in Britain*. It found that higher-level white-collar and professional women were less likely to return to work simply because of the money. They were '. . . more likely to report that their maternity pay or leave period had ended or that they had returned to work through personal choice. This was particularly the case for women who had been employed in the public sector.'

Professional women were the most likely to return full-time, remain in their pre-baby job and go back to the same employer.

And those whose employers offered over and above the statutory minimum maternity rights were more likely to return to work. Extra benefits tend to be conditional upon return to work, of course.

Of the full-time professionally employed women who returned to work within eight or nine months of their baby's birth, 65 per cent came back full-time and 35 per cent part-time. The PSI report continued: 'All but one full-time returner stayed in professional work. The one woman who did not return to work at this level had moved into managerial or administrative work. Similarly, all but three of the professionals who took up part-time work on their return remained in professional work. The three part-time workers who left professional employment moved down occupationally.'

This is how actress Patricia Hodge describes the move back from full-time motherhood to working again.

> *I was so totally taken by this new life I almost lost myself. It was actually a relief when I went back to work to find I still had the skills I used to have and that people still wanted me. I got this little buzz of adrenalin which was my own life beckoning. But now I had a child so that had to be taken into account. I couldn't bear to leave Alexander, who was only six weeks old when I took him on location to Ibiza. I was often the last person on the set at night, had to go back to the hotel to feed and settle the baby and be up again at 5.30, also getting the baby up.*

Your own life will beckon, but of course your life as a whole is now different and there may be changes you want to make to accommodate the new you. Your spare time has disappeared. When you have a new baby, it's hard to imagine how you'll ever find the time to do anything for yourself again. And, although the fog does clear, working mothers still have a job and a half, even with the best of childcare.

Juggling is everything at this stage. Ask yourself whether you want to change the way you work, whether your daily routine could be altered to make things run better. A lot will depend on your hours, your partner's hours and on your childcare arrangements.

If very odd hours or lots of foreign trips are an integral part of your job, then presumably you'll have thought of this when you planned your pregnancy and either decided on a complete change of job or opted for a live-in nanny. But for most professional women used to going that extra mile for the sake of their work, it's likely to be less cut and dried than that. Executive woman is rarely a clock-watcher: her job is more than a means of making money for her.

Susie, a university lecturer, said:

'My work just isn't like that. Nine to five? What's that? The combination of research and teaching means that it always spills over into the evenings, the weekends and the holidays. If I find I'm clear, you can be sure a student will knock on my door with a problem, either to do with his work or something more personal. When you're drying tears or listening to angst, you can't say "Sorry, my shift's over now. If you want to jump from the clock tower, I can't help you." Of course, it's chaos and once I had a baby, I found chaos, other than what she created, wasn't on. I resorted to notices on my door, which I'd stick up, saying "Back tomorrow", about an hour before I was due to go. Devious, but that way I survived.'

You may want to change your hours, cut down the business trips, cut out working at home. There's something to be said for sorting this out first, as long as you take care to assure your boss that you do mean business and that you are committed to your job, although you want to change slightly the way you do it. So if the problem is something as concrete as having so much travel in your job that you'd normally be spending regular nights away from home or that you work very erratic hours, sort it out in a special appointment before you go back to work.

Have some suggestions yourself: don't go in just to ask for things. Have something to offer, something to trade. There may be another area you can move into, another responsibility you can take on instead. All this is another good reason for staying in touch during your maternity leave! If your company is embarking on a new project there may be a slot in it which would be just the job for you and your baby. Or you may know of a colleague who would like to take on more foreign trips and would happily hand over to you work you'd now rather do. Give it some thought before you go in and have something written down to show your boss, if it seems appropriate. Don't expect an answer immediately: he hasn't spent several weeks thinking of how to adapt your job as you have. And that's another reason for going in to see him well ahead of time.

Sharon's job in publishing involved lots of transatlantic trips with spells in the company's New York offices.

'There was no way I could continue with that job. I'd have been a stranger to my own son. I always feel a twinge of envy when I see how close he is to his nanny, as it is. I can't help that, but I can help the endless travel. The woman who was my boss at the time had children of her own and she was very sympathetic. I thought she wouldn't be because she really had a hard time bringing them up when they were little. There'd been no maternity leave then and she'd been at home editing texts for really basic money. I rather expected her to take that "if it was good enough for me, it's good enough for you" line. But she didn't. She listened, questioned me about how committed I was to the company and told me to hold tight for a month or two. I did just that and she juggled things a little and put me in charge of a section dealing with adapting foreign books for the English market – on a par in seniority with what I had before, with the same money and without the travel. That way, we were all satisfied. It paid off for her, as well, because I've stuck with the company, in spite of other offers.'

Many of those professional women who decide on a break of a few years before returning to work when all their children are at school would name the work strait-jacket among their reasons. It's not that they want to give up entirely; it's just that the system seems to be all or nothing. But, if you know your own value and can convince your employer of it, you may find that strait-jacket can be loosened a little to accommodate you.

You may want to alter things quite radically. Taking more work home, not less, may be the answer here. If a lot of your work is desk and phone stuff, how much does it really matter where the desk and phone are? Why not in your study? If it's paperwork, how much does it matter whether it's done in the day or the evening?

Remember that the business world, especially the male-dominated bits of it, is extremely hidebound about this sort of thing. There's a tendency to think a job is something you have to go somewhere every day to do. There's actually been a huge technological revolution in favour of working at home, but looking at the office blocks being thrown up and the fossilised working practices with which we still have to cope, you'd never think it. I have a word processor, a link to my office computer, an answer phone and a fax machine. Why should I get on a train every morning?

Of course, it's important to keep in touch and there's no sense in being away from the hub of things too long. Your boss will think you're in a rut and there's some truth in the saying 'out of sight out of mind' when it comes to promotions. But nevertheless, there's a lot more potential flexibility for the Executive Mother now than the world of work recognises. Some bosses, of course, simply like to have their pawns on the chessboard before them, but others genuinely haven't thought of the alternative. You can open their eyes for them.

Doing part of your work at home doesn't mean you can do without childcare. You can't work and look after a baby. With a baby around you can never absolutely depend on being free to work at a particular time. Babies do sleep of course, but the child who slept beautifully from 10 a.m. to 1 p.m. on Monday will be awake all day Thursday, as bright as a button, while you go frantic thinking of the work you promised to deliver. If you try to handle it without childcare, you have to be prepared to snatch what time you can and rely on your partner for some working time in the evening if you have to.

But for some women, more time at home is the answer, especially if late hours are the norm at your office and you're relying on a childminder rather than a nanny. There's nothing more guaranteed to put your pulse rate up than that dash to pick up the baby at the end of the day, with a traffic jam forming, and your mind racing with images of tearful child, cross childminder and tut-tutting employer. It's all stress you can do without. Other women, with toddlers rather than babies, find that they can manage with just an au pair, if they're allowed to do some proportion of their work at home.

Before embarking on it, though, ask how well you know yourself. Many people say they simply couldn't work from home because they have no discipline. They'd be constantly making themselves a cup of coffee or breaking off to do something round the house. Well, I work from home a lot. Of course, I'm a domestic slut, which helps. I can walk between piles of washing up and simply not see it, if I have a deadline. When it comes to productivity, there's no comparison. Half a day with my head down at home produces far more than a day in an office, with trips to coffee machines, the loo, phone calls, people to talk to, other people's telephone messages to take. But others say the adrenalin of an office keeps them going. It depends on the sort of person you are and no doubt on the type of job too.

Home-working doesn't have a good image. Mention it to most people and they think of little old ladies furiously knitting jumpers which will sell for what they're paid with a couple of noughts on the end. Well, it's not always like that these days. The Amstrad in the sitting room or the study has been a godsend to working mothers, whether they're high- or medium-powered.

The computing industry, not surprisingly, leads the field in offering home-work to professional women. Of course, it's in part necessity, because the industry moves on so fast that two or three years out of the field means expensive retraining. ICI, BP, Grand Metropolitan and Shell are among the big companies who offer home-working.

Perhaps it's not more time at home you need, but just more flexible hours. For example, with childminders and maybe school hours to work round, it may fit your bill to have an earlier start and an earlier finish. The PSI study asked women what changes they would like to see to make it easier for them to return to work after having a baby. Professional women, managers and administrators were the most likely group to suggest changes. Almost a quarter (24 per cent) of professional women wanted flexible working hours – a high figure when you consider that most professionals do not habitually work unsocial hours.

Employers have been forced into it, of course, by those demographic changes we've all been hearing about and they are now more flexible about hours than they were ten years ago. Once again, it's something you're more likely to find in the public sector. The London Borough of Camden, for example, allows employees to work any time between 8 a.m. and 7 p.m., as long as they work what is called the core – the hours between 10 a.m. and 4 p.m., when everyone is at work. It's a minimal disruption to both employer and employee and can make the difference between managing to fix childcare and thus managing to work, and giving up on the whole idea.

Another possibility is job-sharing, perhaps with another mother. Again, although this is quite common in the good old public sector, it's not something private companies have had much to do with and it's not terribly common among the professional classes. According to the Equal Opportunities Commission, around 40 per cent of local authorities offer job shares. Around 2,000 sharers are employed by 56 authorities. Several local authorities say that most of the posts are filled by women coming back from maternity leave.

Investigate it yourself, so you have a detailed suggestion to make. After all, you never know your luck.

Job-sharing sounds ideal, though it's often very hard to find someone whose requirements complement yours exactly. There has to be some give and take, especially with holiday cover. You share all benefits and split the hours. Employers prefer the hand-over to be halfway through the working week so one sharer can update the other. Professionally, it seems popular in teaching, banks and broadcasting. My health visitor, who shared her job with a colleague, was very enthusiastic about it.

Remember, though, working in tandem very much limits your promotion prospects. Still, it can work very well: even better if you both share the same childminder. As with any variant from normal working hours, your problem is convincing your boss that you are just as committed to your job as the woman or man working nine to five Monday to Friday. Of course, you could argue, that with the lengths you're prepared to go to to keep your job, you're even more committed.

There's a special organisation called New Ways to Work, which can help you draw up a plan for job-sharing. It costs £10 for a year's individual membership. They also offer a healthy employer membership. Apart from offering advice, there's the usual service of booklets and factsheets as well as seminars and training sessions for employers interested in making job-shares and the like work. They're a campaigning charity and claim great success, especially among local authorities. They also publish a good manual – details in the bibliography, see page 109.

You may want to consider working part-time for a few years. There's a wrong impression that part-time work on a more or less permanent basis is really for women who want to earn a handy supplement to their partner's salary and that it tends to be non-professional women who go for it. Actually, many executive women find this is just what they want. Many GP and dental practices have part-time partners.

'I'd never thought of medicine as having a part-time possibility until I sat down with my husband and discussed starting a family,' says Hilary, who's a relatively young Executive Mother. She now has two children and she's still only 31.

'The only part-timers I'd come across were semi-retired older GPs who wanted to keep their hand in and were gradually winding down by not taking on any new patients. Then I realised it was a real possibility, because surgery hours vary so much.

'The main reason was because I wanted to be with my children as much as possible without giving up work. It was a matter of an arrangement which would probably last ten years or so. We saw it very much as part of creating a family. I have just the same childcare as, say, a mother working full-time as a teacher. I take baby and toddler to the childminder every day and they stay with her from nine until four. The rest of the day, I'm either at the surgery or at home doing all the extra bits of domestic work which children bring. Of course, I spend some time enjoying myself as well.

'Two of my surgeries are prenatal and postnatal, which is quite a benefit to the practice, because I'm the only woman and there's no doubt that most pregnant women would rather see another woman. I'm sure no one at the practice sees me as a passenger. I do six surgeries a week, which is perhaps slightly more than half a full load and home visits one morning. I only do night-time call-outs if the surgery is desperate or as holiday cover. As long as my husband is in the house with the children, that's fine.

'Our family is complete now and I see the arrangement as really coming into its own when both the children are at school. We'll consider having an au pair then. I'll have time to drive them to school and I'll be there to pick them up, bring them home and still have the energy to play with them. It's true we could have afforded a nanny and I could have kept working full-time, but I really didn't consider it other than as a passing thought to be rejected pretty swiftly. Quality time is only quality if you're not shattered, which, with a full surgery load, I would be. I'm not the most patient or sweet-tempered person in the world and when I'm shattered I'm hell, which is hardly fair on the children . . .'

Britain hasn't yet, as far as I've been able to ascertain, cottoned on to the idea of V-time, which is a voluntary reduction in working hours and, of course, a proportionate reduction in pay. After working like this for a year or so, you have the option of taking up full-time work and full pay again. In New York, more than a thousand people employed by the city itself work V-time. A good idea, but not yet imported.

But something else is beginning to catch on here. Term-time working, which means you have unpaid leave of absence during school holidays, is on offer in some areas of local government:

Oxfordshire County Council and several London boroughs. In the private sector, Boots and Dixons run such schemes too.

Some companies – very few – offer career breaks. The employee, usually a mother wanting to postpone work until the children are at school, takes an unpaid break of up to five years. Most schemes insist on a few weeks' paid refresher training each year. The more promising you are, and the more has been invested in your training, the more likely you are to be eligible for a career break.

Don't undervalue what you have to offer, but it may be you feel that your boss will be put off you if you ask for changes before you come back to work. It's actually unlikely: they want you back and having you on maternity leave has cost them in both pay and talent. But if you think that is the case, then try to carry on as normal first. See how it goes. You may find you can cope, especially if there's some overlap between your partner's hours and yours.

If it doesn't work, don't go in to your boss and simply say it doesn't work and ask him to do something to make it better. Again, it's important to have the ideas and suggestions yourself. Offer him a three-month trial of your new style of working. The disadvantage of this approach is that it's hard to avoid the smell of failure. Whereas if you go in to see him beforehand, having anticipated the problem, you can be positive about your new approach.

Remember, the bottom line is that if you can't come to an agreement and you feel you have to leave, you'll be likely to have to pay back your maternity pay. Agreement on how long you must work before this occurs should have been made before you went on maternity leave.

Apart from permanent or long-term changes to your working pattern, you may need a short-term change. It really does look better if you have all your domestic arrangements well under control – with a week's dry run for preference – before you come back to work. But if things go wrong, as they can, particularly if you're trying to manage the tricky change from full breastfeeding to combining it with bottle-feeding, you may need more time. You could try to arrange, privately, with your boss, a phased return over a month or so, gradually increasing your hours until all is right at home. Some companies, Boots for example, allow women to return part-time during their maternity leave, going full-time by the end of it.

All this of course is assuming that you have a smiling and reasonable boss. Not everyone has. Those who break the law on maternity leave can be dealt with, but the law sadly leaves quite a lot of leeway. And bosses who follow it to the letter can cause a crisis in your career. As we saw in Chapter 3, where it's not 'reasonably practicable' to give back a woman's original job, an employer is still considered to have fulfilled his part of the deal if he offers reinstatement on 'terms and conditions not substantially less favourable'. Which could easily mean a completely different job, even though the money might be unchanged. In other words, you could leave as a cook and come back as bottle-washer. It's less likely to happen so dramatically to Executive Mothers, simply because you've probably had professional training for your job and it makes no sense to waste skills. Unless your employer was desperate to get rid of you he'd hardly pay you a brain surgeon's salary and then ask you to sweep the floor. But it does mean you could face subtle role changes or find yourself pushed into an unpopular area because someone else has been doing your job satisfactorily in your absence.

'I left as soon as I could without having to pay back my maternity leave money,' said one Executive Mother who worked for an education authority. Even local government can be far from angelic, it seems.

> 'They didn't change my money, but I left a job with responsibilities and came back to a sideline. Instead of spending part of each week at the coalface, as it were, going round schools and talking to heads, I was stuck in the office following up parental complaints – not my idea of moulding the nation's education service. My work had been divided up among several other officers, which doesn't make for continuity or consistent judgment, but the directors wouldn't accept that.
>
> 'Legally, I couldn't get them for it. I just knew that instead of a job I felt excited about, I had a dull routine. My husband agreed that we could move to another authority's area. He's a teacher and we both managed to get jobs quite quickly. I'm visiting schools again and he's actually got a promotion. It was rocky for the baby, though, because it meant a change of childminder and she really liked the previous one. She's still not as happy as I would like her to be and now she's two, we're thinking of an au pair and playschool combination.'

If you face that problem, grab it by the horns. Of course, you do have the option of leaving, but, as with the previous example, it could mean uprooting more than just yourself. So don't let it become established, if it isn't what you want. Even if you're told that it's simply that you're not up to date on something because of your absence, don't accept it. Update yourself and get your job back on the terms you had, or at least the terms you want. Make sure everyone knows, in every sense, that you're back and you mean business. Go and talk to your boss and make your case, but don't lose your head and threaten to leave. At this stage, it would cost you money, as we've already seen. But make your displeasure clear and if you don't get what you want straight away, say you'd like a date by which you'll be back to normal. Suggest the date after which, according to your company rules, you'd no longer have to pay back your maternity money. He'll get the message. Remember, you're valuable.

Relaunching completely and going self-employed or freelancing is another possibility. Read my chapters on childcare and a handbook on setting up your own business.

However you return to work, as you were or in some other form, you will have to deal with other people's reactions to your change in status. As well as your own, of course. You may feel torn in two at first. You may even feel heartless because you've left your baby at home, but that will pass in a few days as you realise your baby is well cared for and you are enjoying your work. A part of you which has been dormant for a while will come back to life.

Of course, your colleagues may all be thoroughly pleased for you. For some other women, after all, you'll be an example of what they hope to do themselves. But there are still a few male oiks about who think that a woman's place is in the home and a mother's place is on the other end of her baby's bib strings. I think executive women can rise above all that, knowing full well that his place is in the cave. If it's the boss who's like that, then of course you really do have problems. Either make him forget it by never asking for any concessions or try to convert him. Good luck.

But your problem is more likely to be with peers who rather wish you would go away and be a full-time mother. There's more than one factor at work here. In some cases, of course, they just want you out of the way, especially if you've got a job they want or you're nearer than they are to one they want. But there are career women who feel unnerved by another woman who seems to have done it all. You manage family and job with what seems to them enviable efficiency. They haven't seen you hammering on the supermarket door just before the 8 p.m. close, remember. Older women in your office may envy you your maternity leave and pay, a perk they never had. So beware of the colleague who will put down your lost contract, your mistake, your absentmindedness to lack of commitment. It's often sugar-coated in something like: 'It must be awful to have to come into this place when you'd far rather be at home.' Tell her or him you choose to come into this place. And then of course, there's the behind your back 'How can she leave them? I couldn't do it, you know.'

You know your child is being well cared for and that she has a happy mother, which is important for her. You know that behind your return to work is a bundle of reasons including wanting to, independence, money, interest, which you needn't explain to anyone else. They'll soon get used to it and see you as a colleague, not a returning mother.

'I always felt I had something to prove, which I suppose was that motherhood hadn't addled my brain or made me less keen on my job . . .' That, or something like it, was said to me by almost every working mother I talked to.

While you're proving it, sort out what you're going to do about staying in touch with your children's carer during the day. Mothers at work are often suspected of being unable to forget what's happening at home or at the childminder's house. Some mothers with nannies find it hard not to phone. Others find they can only concentrate on working if they banish all thoughts of home and children from their heads. You'll find out soon enough what sort of mother you are. Remember, if you have a qualified nanny at home, it's a fellow professional you're checking up on all the time. She knows what she's doing, she really does. And you've left instructions to phone you if anything goes wrong.

If you are the sort who wants to stay in touch, ration yourself strictly to one phone call halfway through the day if you can manage it. Nanny will appreciate that and so will your colleagues, who could live without your oohs and aahs of delight over the news of Patrick's first potato print. Your nanny may prefer to phone you once a day, not at a fixed time. That way she's less tied. She may have to take the child out somewhere when you usually call. And you're less likely to be worried than if you phone and no one replies. If you have a childminder, try not to phone unless it's an emergency. She probably has her hands full with several children and if she took phone calls from all their mothers, she'd never be able to cope. It's almost certain she's a mother herself, so she'll do all the worrying for you!

And a word about the Executive Mothers who decide not to be executive any longer. Some of them intend to go back to work, but simply find they can't do it. Some dedicated careerists call it blackmail by guilt, but many women find they are happier taking time out and doing the job of child-rearing as professionally as they were used to handling their earlier job. Some worry about nannies and childminders. Others just find they enjoy their baby too much to hand her over. As usual, there are other countries where this problem is handled better than in the UK. In Sweden, for example, you can take up to 18 months off and still come back to your job. Here, the usual maternity leave doesn't even allow for the recommended breastfeeding time.

You can't know how you will feel until it happens, but be prepared and remember that you could have to pay back some of your maternity pay to your company if you don't return to work. An excellent book on the subject of high-powered career women who choose full-time mothering is *Our Treacherous Hearts*, by Rosalind Coward, published by Faber & Faber.

7

Someone You Can Trust: Deciding to go for childcare

This is where you start hearing the clicking of tongues from male colleagues and your baby's grandmothers, because childcare is one of those subjects guaranteed to get everyone going. Feelings about it run very high, so don't expect your choice to be universally admired. You'll please one grandma, but not the other, and meet approval and disapproval in equal measure whatever you do. The main thing is to please you and your child. You'll do that by thinking about it well in advance and maybe even by trying and abandoning one or two methods before you settle down to what suits you both.

With only a few weeks between the birth and your return to work, you can't leave making firm arrangements until you're clutching a damp little bundle which needs changing, feeding and cuddling by someone loving and competent. Choosing childcare involves waiting lists, interviews and visits to childminders' homes and nurseries, so it's best to use your pre-birth maternity leave to sort it out.

This chapter makes the assumption that you will need childcare from someone other than yourself, though I've included the experience of one woman who changed her mind and went back home to do the job herself. Even if you choose to work from home, you still need another carer there, whether it's a minder or the child's father, who can take over when work needs all your attention. We'll cover the sorts of care available, the general picture of how British working mothers cope and how different methods suit different cases.

First, a word of comfort. There will be moments of crisis, as anyone who has sat next to a working mother in an office will tell you. It always starts with a phone call, of which you hear only one side. Conversations with au pairs are the most nerve-wracking, because while the professional working woman tries to stay calm and use clear, slow English, the mother can't wait to shake the poor bewildered girl to whom she's entrusted her beloved children.

'Are they both okay?'

'You're where? Give me the number and I'll ring you back.'

'You weren't supposed to take them on the bus.'

'You should have explained your English wasn't very good.'

'He's being sick? There in the bus depot?'

'I'm coming round straight away.'

It's fraught. You may entrust the care of your child to another woman for a few hours, but the responsibility is right with you, at your desk. The fact is that au pairs do get homesick; nannies do fall in love and want to move in with boyfriends; nurseries do suffer outbreaks of headlice; even under the most watchful eye, a child can damage itself; grandmas do have different ideas from you and tense rows can develop over whether your baby should be given a dummy just because you always had one; playgroup members will occasionally try to bury one of their lot in the sandpit. One story, maybe apocryphal, tells of a nanny who asked for maternity leave.

The comfort? The accidents are nearly always minor and they're not your fault. You've made the best arrangement you could. And who's to say baby wouldn't have tried to swallow that plastic truck just the same if you'd been around?

Jennifer, a sister in a small private hospital, says:

'My husband obviously thought I should stay at home once Jasper was born. He kept saying that childcare would cost about a third of my salary, which was right in one sense, but I didn't see it that way. I saw it as costing about a sixth of our joint salaries. I don't work only for the money. Anyhow, we fixed a weekly nanny, a young girl who'd done some sort of BTEC course in caring, and decorated a bedroom for her. We spent a week looking after the baby together before I went back to the hospital and she seemed fine. But a couple of weeks later, she left because she was homesick, which was rather ridiculous – home was only around 15 miles up the road.

'The experience frightened me off a bit and I came home again – my husband's attitude was very much "I told you so" – until

Jasper was 18 months old when we found a childminder, a woman who'd been left by her husband with two young boys and found it was a good way to look after them and make money by looking after others as well. Because I'd taken so much time out, I had to pay back some of my maternity money and when I did return I had to take a lower level job for a while until I was promoted again. If you don't want to work nights, nursing jobs are more restricted. But she's been super, never once bothered me at work. I'm sure there are crises, but I don't get to hear about them. I trust her.'

Before you decide on your sort of childcare, sit down with your partner and list your requirements. It'll come down to a compromise and a juggle in the end, but you might as well start off knowing what you'd like in an ideal world!

Your hours (both yours and your partner's):
Are they full-time? Is there flexi-time? Do you start early and finish early or the opposite? Or are your hours quite unpredictable? Can you change them? Is there any possibility of doing some work from home, if you'd like to? What about your travelling time to work? Do you ever have to be away from home overnight or for several days at a stretch?

Support:
Have you any nearby relatives whom you trust and who would like to help out? Is your partner's job more flexible or less well-paid than yours?

Where you live:
Are you near a nursery school? Is there public transport to your house if you decide on a daily nanny? If you decide on a shared nanny or a childminder, how long will it take you to do the morning child run? How good are you at getting up in the mornings?

Your budget:
How much will you have to pay for childcare? Are you willing to cut down other expenses? Remember, as Jennifer said, that if you have a career, there's no reason to calculate childcare as a percentage of the mother's salary alone. It's a percentage of the joint income of you and your partner.

A statistic or two:
45 per cent of the babies of full-time working mothers are cared for in the baby's home, 63 per cent in someone else's home,

two per cent in a private nursery, one per cent in a workplace nursery and so few in local authority nurseries, they don't show up in percentaged figures. The childminder is the most popular choice.

Remember, when it comes to totting things up, that if you have two children born close together, you'll be paying for two lots of pre-school childcare.

In Britain you're battling against the odds, whatever childcare arrangements you come to. In spite of noises made over the last few years about Government and industry wanting to encourage more women into the workplace, very little has been done about it. You've no doubt heard of the demographic time-bomb, which means the number of school-leavers is in steep decline and that, in spite of the jobless figures, the number of people working is expected to rise a million above the 1987 figure by 1995. The Government estimates that three-quarters of the rise will be women. And yet, not a lot has been done to help. Most women still struggle and juggle to get back to work in Britain.

In Scandinavia and Eastern Europe, the view is that bringing up the next generation is the responsibility of society as a whole. The British point of view is still very much that you decide to have babies, so you make the sacrifices involved in their care.

In Denmark, 48 per cent of children under three have a publicly funded childcare place. In Belgium and France, the figure is 20 per cent. We're at the bottom of the league below even Germany (3 per cent), Greece (4 per cent) and Portugal (6 per cent). And although things are better for the three-and-overs we're still bottom of the Euro-league, except for Portugal, for publicly funded places. At the top of the league are Belgium and France with 95 per cent of children aged three and over in publicly funded places.

In Sweden, a deliberate childcare policy brought about a rise in the employment of women with school-age children from 27 per cent in 1965 to 82 per cent in 1983. The Swedish parliament decided that every child of pre-school age with parents either working or studying should have a childcare place. And in other countries, there's tax relief on childcare too, something British mothers are still battling for. No wonder only 27 per cent of British women with children below school age work outside the home. It rises sharply to 76 per cent with a youngest child of 11 or over.

The CBI conducted a Gallup poll of women between 25 and 45 who were not at work. Sixty-four per cent wanted to return.

Four-fifths of those wanting to work were prevented from doing so because of looking after small children at home. And 28 per cent said they would go back immediately if satisfactory childcare arrangements could be made. According to the Midland Bank, one of the few private companies to have its own childcare facilities, 70 per cent of women do not come back after maternity leave. Obviously this covers a lot of non-executive lower earners, but it's still a pretty devastating figure.

Let's take a look at one profession. In 1990, the Law Society published a report from its Working Party On Women's Careers. Law is a career which now attracts a lot of women. By 1986, 44 per cent of solicitors admitted were women. After admittance, things start slowing down quite dramatically. Only seven of the 127 presidents of local law societies are women. Women are much slower to become partners in law firms and more likely to remain assistant solicitors. The report found that 'a significant and alarming number' of women were taking a temporary break after a few years in spite of the increased intake. And temporary breaks often lead to being permanently behind.

The figures are not encouraging, but an awful lot of women manage somehow. There are lots of organisations which can give you detailed help with finding the right childcare and advise you on cost. They're listed in the back of the book.

In some professions, of course, women have the clout to help themselves. In July 1992, the Bar approved a policy advising chambers to give women barristers a year off to have a baby without losing their right to return to work.

In 1991 the Policy Studies Institute undertook a survey of women in work during pregnancy (*Maternity Rights in Britain*) which revealed that 46 per cent of women wanted more workplace crèches and nurseries – a high figure bearing in mind many professional women work in organisations which don't have a large enough staff for it to be a realistic option. Only two per cent of the women in work after the birth used workplace or private nurseries, which suggests a lot of women aren't getting the childcare of their first choice.

Of course, going back to work after maternity leave isn't right for every woman. Even if you've watched other women coping, you may still feel put off by hearing the Executive Mother who works so late she puts her children to bed via the office telephone. Some women decide on a career break, feeling that the best carer for the baby is its mother or simply that they miss the baby too much.

Jeri was a journalist on a Sunday colour supplement, highly paid with executive powers. Now she's at home with her baby, something she never envisaged.

'Don't regret it at all. I'm always rather amused when I see the "oh, a housewife" look pass over someone's face at a dinner party. Probably it used to pass over my face too. You need pretty high self-esteem not to feel you've opted out, but luckily I've got that. I wasn't expecting to be a home mother at all. I was 32 when I got pregnant and frankly used to the money. The pregnancy was just awful, because my sickness didn't stop at three months. It went on for around seven months and was so bad I had to have leave from work.

'I was losing weight because I couldn't eat without throwing up. I didn't really gain weight until well into the fifth month. I'm naturally very sporty and fit and resented how the baby was making me feel. My body didn't seem my own any longer and when I felt the first movements they were uncomfortable. You're supposed to find it warming and comforting, but I just wished it would stop. I finally went back to work with the sickness under control as long as I ate something bland every two hours. I never want to see a cream cracker again. Of course, although they officially were nice about it at work, there seemed to be doubt in some people's minds about whether I was malingering.

'When maternity leave eventually started, I did all the buying and preparing for the baby, but it was the height of summer and the main thing on my mind was how uncomfortable and hot I felt all the time. It makes me sound like the world's most heartless mother, but there was absolutely no bonding with the baby before birth in my case. Afterwards it was very different. I took maximum maternity leave and made an arrangement with the editor to return to work gradually, starting part-time.

'It was very hard. I missed Harry like mad and I worried even though I knew he was safe with my mother. I tried to make the part-time arrangement permanent, but was told that wasn't on, so I came back full-time. I really tried and the office was glad I was back, but the fact was I had become a clock-watcher. I couldn't wait to get back each evening.

'The worst thing was the change in Harry from Monday to Friday. On Monday mornings, after we'd been together all weekend, he was very tearful and sad to see me set off for work. By Friday morning, he was as different again and could hardly bother to say goodbye. That's what did it in the end. It hurt me so much to leave him. I was actually feeling envious of my own mother, as well as guilty at the demands I was making on her. Harry was almost a year old. I'd given it a fair crack of the whip and I handed in my notice to come home full-time. It's been wonderful. We want another baby and, assuming we can do it financially, I'll stay at home until they're both at school. Then I'll go back to magazines. It doesn't feel like a failure at all. That's my choice. And it's amazing what you don't spend when you're not a career woman!'

But most professional women go back to work before their children are at school. In the next chapter, we look at the sorts of childcare you can choose from.

8

The Hand That Rocks Your Baby's Cradle: Different sorts of childcare

The time to think about childcare is early on in your pregnancy. You won't have the time you need once the baby is born. Here are details of different sorts of childcare.

Childminders

Since the Nursery and Childminders Act of 1984, things have been tightened up by the local authorities, who keep a register of minders in their areas. The childminder will have applied to be registered with your local authority and her home will have been visited by the local social services department and checked for safety. Once minding is underway, there may be regular visits from the department to check all is well. The number of children a childminder is allowed to look after varies from local authority to authority, but a common combination is three under-fives, only one of whom may be less than 12 months old. The three-to-one ratio compares favourably to nurseries, which may be especially important while your child is a baby. It's the nearest thing to one-to-one care you'll get without a nanny.

Your local social services department will provide a list of vacancies with registered childminders in your area – assuming there are any. Phone them for help. Then, when you've got a name, arrange to visit her. If there's a shortage of registered minders, you could always advertise for a woman who would like to become a minder and persuade her to become registered. The drawback here is that many local authorities take an age to do the registration. Make sure you find someone near you. Remember you or your partner has to take the child to the minder's before you go to work every morning.

Mothers who use childminders seem to have fewest horror stories to tell. And very important to most of the mothers I know is the fact that a minder is nearly always a mother herself. Childminders are less likely to flit about the place than nannies, because they have ties such as their partners' jobs and their children's schools. Most of them are happy to have the chance to work from home, so once you've found a place, the chances are it will be for good. Many mothers like the idea of a home environment for the child, while feeling pleased it's not their home. They don't want any confusion over who is mummy and who is minder. Unlike having grandma in charge for the day, having a childminder combines a business deal with a home environment and many parents feel happiest with this.

In most areas, social services will arrange cover with another registered minder if the childminder is ill. But if your child is ill, the minder may well refuse to look after him for the sake of her other charges. Most childminders appreciate the convenient hours of their job, so if your own is unpredictable or involves shifts, which means you can't pick your child up at a particular time, this may not be the form of care for you.

Childminding was the major change in childcare in the 1980s. To find out what childminding costs and how it varies in different parts of the country, contact the National Childminding Association, whose details are in the back of the book. Expect to pay a minimum of £55 a week (November 1992 figure) and around £70 in London. In case your child should have an accident in the minder's house, check her insurance policy first. Members of the National Childminding Association should be able to show you an up-to-date policy. Otherwise, check that your minder is insured through the local authority.

Under the Nursery and Childminders Act, a childminder is anyone who looks after a child under school age for any period of more than two hours in six days. A would-be childminder has to answer questions about herself and other adults in the household; questions about health, family and whether any of her own children have been in care. A doctor's reference is required. Her house is visited and checked for size, safety and suitability.

The Act is open to individual interpretation by each local authority, so the vetting procedure varies round the country. Ring your local Social Services and ask what theirs is and find out how many children each minder is allowed to look after. A registered child-minder will be visited regularly by an officer from the authority's under-fives team. Again, ask how often this actually occurs.

Heather, a University librarian, says:

'Childminder every time for me. I wanted someone as near to a mother as possible and a family situation. The thought of my baby being "lost" in a sea of other babies at a nursery was frightening. I had this vision of her just being left in a corner to play with toys. And I'm afraid that when my husband and I talked it over neither of us really wanted to share our house with a nanny. We didn't really have the room either, because our spare bedroom is really for his two daughters from his previous marriage who come and stay at weekends. The last thing we wanted to do was alienate them – we considered we'd been pretty lucky that they were pleased about the baby.

'A day nanny was a possibility but I didn't know anyone who'd tried that whereas lots of people seemed happy with their minders. I left it rather late to ask for one, rather assuming they were there for the having. The social services department said there was nothing doing at the moment, but then I heard of a place coming up from another new mother – one of the many advantages of all the extra friends you acquire at prenatal classes. The other good thing about a minder was that away from our home I felt there was less danger of the baby getting confused between mummy and minder. Of course, you can't impose your ideas on a minder. You have to be reasonably pragmatic and fit in with her routine – she's looking after two or three children after all. If you're too fussy you can find yourself spending your weekend correcting all the habits the baby has picked up during the week, which is confusing for everyone.

'And you have to get up early in the morning, get self and baby ready and drive to the minder before you even set off for work. It's not the easiest of options. Our minder had children of her own, so I felt quite easy leaving our baby with her. In fact, for all their qualifications, I don't know if I'd have felt as happy leaving a baby with a young nanny. Perhaps that's my prejudice, but knowing how inept I was when I came out of hospital, it's hard to believe a girl ten or 12 years younger would be much better. Another benefit – the house is tidier during the week, no child-messes around. All hell breaks loose on Saturday morning, but that's another matter.'

Nurseries

All nurseries should be registered with the local social services department, so go there for a list, which should include those run by the Council, private nurseries, community nurseries and even workplace nurseries. You'll have to check with the individual nursery for costs. Some eminent child experts are against nurseries for children under one year old, though in the United States they're all the rage. These experts believe that very young children need to be cared for by one person and some even claim that adult personality disorders can be traced to diverse carers in the earliest months.

Certainly, visiting a nursery towards the end of the day, when carers don't have enough hands to cuddle all the fretful tots, makes you wonder if this form of care isn't better confined to children who are rather nearer school age.

The big advantages are that nurseries are usually open all the year and that they offer the best social life for your child, assuming she's old enough to need one. And they usually have the best supply of toys and range of things to do, depending on the staff ratio. Again, because nurseries are open between 8 a.m. and 6 p.m., they aren't for you if you and your partner have irregular hours. And remember, the nursery may not be on your route to work.

Council nursery places are envied, not least because you know there's a minimum standard. They usually cost less than £10 a week, have NNEB (National Nursery Examination Board) trained staff and a ratio of one to five children over two and one to three children under two. But the fact is that most places go to cases of special need and a career mother would be very lucky indeed to find a spare place, even though, according to DHSS figures, there are around 27,000.

Of course, you may be lucky if you work for a big employer and find a nursery on the premises. The tax on employers' subsidies for childcare was removed for workplace nurseries in 1990. It was a fine example, but don't get too hopeful: there are only about 120 workplace nurseries in the UK (two-thirds in the public sector) providing places for 3,000 children. Hospitals and universities lead the field here. Usually, there's a cost-sharing scheme between employer and employees. Some women grab the chance to visit their child at lunchtime and even to breastfeed. Others find it rather confusing to have their child so near to them when they are in work mode and would rather keep the two worlds separate.

Remember, when you leave your job, your baby leaves the nursery. Community nurseries are a smashing idea, but because they often depend on parental help and a sympathetic local authority, there aren't many of them. You have to be in the catchment area and costs are often levied according to income. There's usually a management committee made up of parents and local authority representatives and the premises are often provided by the authority at a low rent. Because they depend heavily on parental input, they often collapse. The advantage is that you can have a real say in how the place is run, but so can everyone else! And remember you may be called upon to help.

Which really leaves only one realistic choice of nursery, the private kind, for which you'll probably pay at least £500 a month for each child. Between 1988 and 1991, places in private and voluntary nurseries in Britain more than doubled to 75,000. They're nearly always businesses, though some charitable ones do exist. Make sure you check them thoroughly and are quite happy with what you see. Ask about staff qualifications – there may be none – and hang around long enough to check the staff-to-children ratio is what they claim it is. Although pieces of paper aren't everything when it comes to childcare, you will feel happier to know the staff hold the NNEB certificate or have a similar childcare qualification. And use the council nursery staffing ratio – one staff member to five children over the age of two and one to every three children under two – as a guide. Ask about first-aid facilities and training, too. And, if you don't know anyone whose child goes to the nursery, ask to be put in touch with another working mother. If the nursery won't oblige, strike it off your list. Above all, use your eyes. A gang of toddlers can't be press-ganged into putting on a good show for visitors, so you should get a pretty clear picture of what goes on. You can't be too careful, so don't feel foolish when you ask to see the toy-boxes. Remember, this place has to be a very good second best to home.

There's also part-time nursery care, which may be just what you want if you've had a spell at home with children and are thinking of working part-time or if you've come to an arrangement with your mother or another relative for the rest of the time. There are private Montessori schools, which cost quite a bit but fit some parents' bill exactly. They take children from the age of two and a half for anything from half a day to a full (short) school day. The emphasis is on independence and learning. Local education authorities also run nursery schools for children aged between three and five. They're free, but most offer only a two-and-a-half hour morning and places are hard to come by.

If a nursery is for you, start looking early and get your child's name down on the waiting list. Find out what the cost includes and ask about the meals.

Sue, who works in the City and uses a London nursery, says:

'I think a lot of women use childminders because they feel guilty, so they try to provide something as like home as possible. Both my children attended a private nursery. In fact we moved to be near to it. There's much more stimulus and socialising for them. They've never been at all difficult with relatives and friends, because they're used to mixing. They got off to a flying start at school, because they already knew how to play with other children and were just more socially aware. You know they're with professionally trained people and there's no worry about staff illness. It's definitely on a business footing, which is a help when it comes to saying what you want and checking up on things. It's much harder to feel easy about doing that in someone else's home.'

Nannies

Two women talk about their nannies:

'There's simply no other way we could do it. We needed full cover. I have to be able to stay late at work if there's a crisis. I travel regularly too. My husband's hours are more regular, but why should he come home after a day's work and have to start feeding and bathing if I don't? Sometimes it feels as if the nanny costs the earth, but she's worth it for being so flexible. People laugh at the idea of "quality time" with your children and I suppose it does sound very yuppie, but that's how it feels. I'm all theirs at the weekend.'

'Um, I hate having to tell people I've got a nanny, because it sounds so ridiculous. I'm a single parent, so they rather raise their eyebrows there too. I suppose I'm rather neurotic, always on the phone to her, so she puts up with a lot. She's become a friend, actually, and I don't know what I'll do if she leaves. Why not a childminder? I wanted the baby, who has enough to put up with not having a father, to have as stable a time as possible. That meant being cared for at home.'

Well, you can forget Mary Poppins. Although the Duchess of York did spark a vogue for uniformed nannies, products of colleges such as Norland and Princess Christian, few people today have the Julie Andrews version in their nursery. A walk in the park will not reveal lots of starched matrons pushing large, well-sprung prams, but you may spot a few casually dressed young women meeting each other with their push-chair charges.

For the career woman who needs to be able to give her all to her job, a nanny is hard to match. If you never know when you may have to stay late at work, if you sometimes have to get on a plane and just go, you need to know that there's flexible, 24-hour if necessary, care in the home. Of course, you'll pay for it, not only in money and loss of family privacy, but in time and effort spent before the baby arrives, while you look for the right person.

Ask yourself how important qualifications are to you. If they are, then you need a nanny with the National Nursery Examination Board qualification, which means she has trained for two years. Of course, a nanny may be a former nursery teacher or simply someone with experience. There are day nannies, weekly nannies, live-in nannies and shared nannies. If sharing appeals, try an advert in your local NCT newsletter. It's important to get someone you like, because, to some extent or another, you'll be living with her. Live-in nannies are cheaper (a minimum of £100 a week compared to £200 for dailies), but you have to provide a room and meals. Find out what the Income Tax and National Insurance arrangements are from your local Inland Revenue PAYE department and your local branch of the DHSS. Or consult your accountant, because the chances are you will end up paying your live-in nanny's tax and NI contribution, if you pay her more than 'the lower earnings limit'. It applies to anyone you employ in your home, so calling your nanny a mother's help makes no difference!

Basically this means: you deduct her NI contribution and income tax from her pay and you pay the employer's NI contribution. Every quarter you work out the total of your contributions, her contributions and her tax and you pay all three to the Inland Revenue direct.

Your local office of the Inland Revenue will give you what you need: a simplified deduction card, simplified tax tables, National Insurance contribution tables, and a book of payslips to send with your quarterly cheque.

But to set against this is that live-in nannies are the most flexible form of childcare. Most get their free time at the weekends when you're having your 'quality time' with the baby. If you find you need her to be on child-duty Saturday morning, you can always trade this against an extra night off during the week. Live-in nannies are never late to work in the mornings, either, which is a big plus when you're dashing off to work.

You have more privacy with a daily or weekly nanny, of course. And as she has a life outside your house, you're less likely to have to act as a shoulder to cry on when there are problems. And you save on space, though your weekly nanny may not appreciate her room being turned into the weekend guest room. Some families share nannies, with one parent taking the child to the other family's house for shared care. It's more profitable for the nanny and is cheaper for the parents. The main drawback is that arrangements can become complicated. Who pays more and how much more? What happens when one side pulls out?

But first catch your nanny. The chances are you will have to advertise, unless you can find one freshly trained through a Further Education college. The trade magazine of the live-in nanny world is *The Lady*, so you could advertise there as well as in *Nursery World*, your local Job Centre, local paper and newsagents' windows. There's a nannies section in Yellow Pages too.

Allow yourself lots of time. In the advert, say what you're looking for. If you run a kennels, say you'll need a dog-lover. If cigarettes infuriate you, specify non-smoker (don't be fooled by someone who says she's a smoker but she won't do it in the house. She will.) Say how old the children are and that she will have her own room. Don't go into too much detail: you may put off the very person you'd get on with best. But do say enough to sift out the obvious no-hopers. And if your working hours are odd, say so.

When you've got the list down to a few, fix some interviews. There should be at least four of you there: you, the nanny, your partner and the child. Watch how she relates to the child. Talk about how she does the job and how you want the child to be looked after. If you have very strong views on child-rearing, an experienced woman with her own very strong views may not be the best bet. Without laying down specific rules (you can do that nearer the time) give an idea of your views on your child's discipline and diet. Nannies who keep babies quiet with laudanum and gin may be no longer with us, but those who do the same with chips and sweets most definitely are. Give a clear outline of duties and hours. Do you expect her to do housework or cooking? Do you have other people working in the house?

And be fair – fill her in on the sort of work you do and how long it keeps you away from home. Ask her about her previous jobs and why she likes nannying. Find out if she likes a formal carry-on, being called 'nanny' and so on, or if she'd rather be part of the family. Let her see her room and ask her if she likes it. Be prepared to respect her privacy within the rules you've laid down. Make quite clear what you will and will not stand in the way of visitors. Remember she's a working woman too and entitled to decent conditions of service. Let her see the baby's room and any play areas. And, no matter how well you seem to hit it off, don't offer the job on the spot. You need to talk about it with your partner.

Insist on references. There have been cases of nannies who have assaulted their charges. Ask to see the NNEB certificate and remember letters of reference can be forged. Ask for referees' telephone numbers and ring them up. If there's any hesitation on the part of the nanny, alarm bells should ring!

When you offer a nanny a job, make sure the hours, holidays and duties are spelled out, preferably on paper. Imagine installing someone in your house and finding out only too late that she has a different idea from you about why she's there. It's a good idea to draw up some form of contract with your nanny – not legally binding, but useful. Set out hours, work, holidays and any house rules you may have about smoking, boyfriends, etc. Check your household insurance and, if you're letting her drive your car, make sure she's covered. And ask to see her licence. If she's young, ask her for her parents' address and phone number just in case of emergency. Remember, she's looking after your baby, but she may need a little looking after herself.

Before the day comes to leave your baby with the nanny, give her a written guide to the baby with all his personal quirks and details of feeding. Some women like to be more specific and leave a timetable for the day. Don't forget phone numbers where she can reach you, your partner and the doctor.

Au Pairs

Well, for all the jokes, they come cheaper than nannies and many families find they're interesting and fun to have around the place. Children often love them, because they tend to be young and informal. That's the good news. The bad news is that they're in-experienced, short-stay, and sometimes horribly unreliable. As well as probably having very little English, they often get homesick. Having said that, they can be just what you need – if you're lucky – and many people manage quite successfully with a string of au pairs over several years.

You are obliged to fix English lessons for your au pair and to give her some spending money and a decent room of her own. Au pairs usually stay for six months to a year and because they're often very young they may be better with children than babies. By the way, at the moment, because of some fluke in our immigration rules, au pairs have to be female if they come from outside the EC, though this is under Home Office review. Under the Treaty of Rome, EC citizens have complete freedom of movement, so EC au pairs can be male or female.

By Home Office definition an au pair is unmarried, 'aged 17–27 inclusive and without dependants . . . a national of a Western European country'. He or she 'may come into the UK to learn the English language and to live for a time as a member of an English-speaking family'. Au pairs are normally expected to work around five hours a day, or thirty hours a week, so they're not suitable for full-time childcare. Many women who have had a nanny swap to an au pair once the children are at school. Talk to an au pair agency and ask them to send you some written details about the scheme before you plunge in.

The Immigration and Nationality Department of the Home Office, or the Central Bureau for Educational Visits and Exchanges, whose details are in the address list, will answer any queries on au pairs. There are very many agencies, some of which specialise in au pairs from a particular country. You may hear about a good agency from a friend. They advertise in Yellow Pages, *The Lady*, *Nursery World* and all the parenting magazines. You may prefer to find an au pair by personal recommendation, using contacts abroad.

One Executive Mother said:

'I started off with high hopes of working from home and looking after the baby. I thought it would be easy because as a private accountant I can vary my hours and I could just see myself sitting there at my figures, occasionally reaching over to rock a sleeping baby. Actually, it wasn't far wrong, for the first few months. I was breastfeeding, the workload was modest and Simon did sleep a lot during the day.

'Gradually though, he was sleeping less and less and though I didn't take on any more work, I was getting less done and found myself dumping the baby on my husband in the evening so I could work. The result was two exhausted adults and one bright-eyed baby. I didn't want to give up the dream altogether, so we got in touch with the British Council about an au pair. There's space in the house and it seemed just the right number of hours. We're on with our second one now and, touch wood, they've been very good, though we had to get firm with the first one on the subject of smoking. Simon adapted well, because she was always around anyhow and he didn't seem to notice when mummy-time faded into au pair-time and back again. We had to be quite strict about it, so that I could have three or four hours straight run at my work every weekday. After that, her time is her own. It's actually really good to have someone about during the day, even if it means being there for their crises. I have a 'please interrupt' rule, because it's not like having a fully qualified nanny around the place.'

Those are the main types of childcare outside the family. Before you make a final decision, it may be worth chatting to your boss and to your personnel department, if there is one, about possible adjustments to hours or even contributions to childcare. The company may be willing to help a valued member of staff come back fully confident that her baby is in good hands.

When it comes to handover time, do it gradually. If it's a nanny or an au pair, it's much easier because she can be around for a week or so, getting used to the baby. And the child will realise she has two carers not one and that nanny isn't chasing mummy out of the house. For your own peace of mind, let your nanny be in charge for a couple of days while you're still at home, just so you know she can do it. Learn to trust your nanny, especially if you're working at home. Constant sightings of mummy will be unsettling for the baby and will probably make the nanny nervous. So resist the temptation to put your head round the door every time you hear a yell.

With a childminder or day nursery, take your baby in by degrees, maybe a morning a week and gradually build up. It avoids that awful feeling of desertion – for both of you. In all cases, leave emergency phone numbers with the carer.

Whoever your carer is, she'll be a better carer (and you'll be a more relaxed mother) if she's had some first-aid training. St John

Ambulance Brigade does first-aid courses in some parts of the country. Check with your local branch.

At the end of the day, when you're home from work or calling at the childminder's, resist the temptation to scoop up your baby, check her all over and bear her off with never a word to the carer. She's been with your child all day, so talk to her and find out what the children have been doing and how she is. This is particularly important with the young nanny, for whom you may be a substitute family to a certain extent. If she has problems, you and your baby will suffer, so make sure you talk.

How much does it all cost? It varies hugely. According to the Policy Studies Institute report, *Maternity Rights in Britain*, 85 per cent of full-time professional women pay for childcare and they pay more than any other group – an average of £44 per week. And of course in Britain we're still waiting for childminding tax allowances.

Then, of course, there's the childminder you don't have to pay, though it still costs you a lot of money. There aren't many fathers who stay at home to look after their children, but they do exist and I was astonished by how many different reasons for doing this househusbands came up with. I came to the conclusion that, just as women feel guilty about leaving their children to go to work, men feel guilty about leaving work and looking after children. In each case, there's a certain role model expected by society and being bucked by the individual. For some couples, it's purely a money decision: the wife earns enough to support the family. But, as childcare rarely costs the equivalent of the entire second income, there's usually another reason.

Sometimes it's that the couple believes parental care is better. But usually, it's that the husband is in some way less than happy with his job and wants a change anyway. And, of course, some men just want to be full-time fathers. I even came across one couple who wouldn't have had a child if full-time fatherhood hadn't been part of the deal. The wife, a publishing editor, was less keen on children than her husband to start with. And she felt that if they opted for a childminder, maternal guilt and the fact that her hours were shorter than her husband's would land her with most of the remaining responsibility. They didn't have room for a live-in nanny.

Derek had had a previous family and said:

'I'd already done it the conventional way round: wife at home, husband returning at 5.30 in the evening, greeted rather like a star turn but actually too tired to act it. And I've had the best of my career too, if I'm being honest about it. At 55, I wasn't going to climb any higher. Frankly, I didn't want to – I've never been driven by the need to prove myself. I've got better things to do.

'But I love children and always thought my first wife had the better side of the bargain. I wanted Alison to have them for herself as well as for my sake. So many women who marry older men either miss out or leave the marriage to start a family with a younger man. And there was the feeling that maybe this time it could work well. In my first marriage there was a certain amount of resentment which seemed to centre on the children. This time, it's very different.

'I love being with Thomas and Alison loves coming home to him. She takes over, full of energy somehow, at the end of the day when I'm beginning to flag. She's still hungry for success in her job. She breastfed Thomas for three months before going back to work, but you could tell she was itching to be back among the action again. She never really stopped, because she kept having book proofs sent to her while she was away. I'd catch her ringing the office from the study extension when I thought she was putting Thomas to bed for a nap. She's totally hooked. And me? Well, looking after children is valuable work, isn't it? It's actually interesting and fulfilling, too. And when the children are at school, I've one or two pet projects I wouldn't mind having a crack at.'

9

Bibs and Bods: the parts other chapters didn't reach

Talking to working mothers is often a hoot. From reading the instructions on the pregnancy test kit ('don't splash the windows') to wangling time off for a school sports afternoon ('leave your jacket on the back of your chair and don't come back boasting about winning the mothers' race'), the Executive Mother will find that life is as funny as it is frantic. In this chapter, you'll find examples of both.

'I thought they just slept and fed. Mine just feeds.'
Nothing can prepare you for sleepless nights, and there's little worse than pacing the nursery floor in the small hours with a small child in your arms knowing that you have to get up and go to work in the morning. Of course, there are the wonder babes who sleep from birth. You know, they have twelve hours sleep a night and a good long nap morning and afternoon. My mother's hairdresser's baby slept so long and late she had to be woken for breakfast, and sometimes for lunch as well.

There are no rules. And, whatever people say about discipline, some very disciplined parents – often very smug parents – of one child find that second time round they have given birth to a nocturnal creature who resists their sacred routine. And then there are those poor souls who are blessed with a sleeping baby, but have a toddler who still wakes up in the middle of the night at the age of three to wander into their bedroom.

From a few days old, my own baby would wriggle and cry if I held her in my arms the way you feel proper babies should be cradled. She was only happy held upright against me and she hated the feeling of being put down in a cot. Many times I would lower her in, holding my breath, only to see her open her eyes and start clapping her hands – hilarious and exasperating all at once.

We'd just got her into a reasonable pattern – well, she was going to sleep at 7 p.m. and waking up at about 4 a.m. for a feed, but that was relatively good – when we moved house. All hell broke loose. We'd decided to use the opportunity to put her in her own room, which was probably too much of a change for her to take. She began waking almost hourly during the evening. I'd always fed her lying down in bed during the night, with those dire warnings from older women of 'rod for your back' ringing in my sleepy ears. But it got me through. It meant I could rest, and even sleep, as Rosie fed.

She gradually stopped the early wakings but still ended up spending the last few hours of the night in our bed. It was impossibly cramped. I was waking up with backache and David was being kicked awake every morning by a fast flurry of baby feet. Something had to be done. We bought a bigger bed.

So, I have no magic solution for this one. There are books, of course, which suggest well-tried methods. It all depends on your energy and your inclinations. Tired career women often desperately need sleep but are too tired to try a new regime which might be damned hard for a week or two. Some women, like me, simply can't or won't leave their baby to cry, though their husbands are often willing to give it a go.

I know couples who have reported success with an over-the-counter sedative for children of a year or more. But I've heard far more stories of babies sleeping with their parents, which is no doubt what nature intended. What worries me is how we'll fit a ten-year-old in the bed. One of my male colleagues, who finishes work around midnight, reports having to clear the bed of three-year-old and eight-month-old every night before clambering in beside his wife.

A friend, who had decided on a two-year career break from her job as a hospital pharmacist, took the baby into bed with her every night because she was terrified of cot death. Her partner, who worked away from home during the week, returned home one weekend armed with the most sophisticated state-of-the-art baby alarm and a lot of determination.

Confusion reigned for some weeks. At one point, my friend, reluctant to upset her partner, but still terribly worried, moved her mattress into the baby's bedroom during the week. Things did settle down eventually, but she still checked the baby every twenty minutes during the evening. She hadn't seen a television advert for months because she was constantly trotting upstairs during the commercial break.

'My Beth does murder sleep . . .'

Sleeplessness, and the general exhaustion that children bring, hits those who commute most of all. Commuting and having a family is very hard work and some women find jobs nearer home. It's not just the early rising which is hard; it's the daily dash to get home before bath-time or bedtime, the sprint to the train in the mornings after a hastily planted kiss on a porridge-spattered forehead.

'Guilt? I felt I was buying my way out of it. Always a cab from the office to the station. Always a Friday night present for Beth to make up for being home late, and to make up for not being able to hand it over until Saturday morning. And the weekends were times for expensive treats. "What would you like mummy to buy?" I asked the question in the toyshop and I asked it in the super-market.

'It wasn't good for my work, either, because I was constantly looking for an early escape, hoping to get a train which would let me do the bathing and goodnight routine, instead of the nanny. On top of that, I was shattered by the nights. Beth slept her full twelve hours in her own cot but she woke for a 3 a.m. feed and I'm not someone who can get by on six or seven hours. I was dragging myself about after a few months of it. We could have moved to London, but neither of us felt we wanted to bring up a family there.

'In the end, I took a job in Tunbridge Wells, where we live, and my husband continued to commute. My salary is slightly down, but we managed to keep the nanny on, not least because walking to work is much cheaper than a British Rail season ticket. Life is good and I may even have the energy for another baby,' said a thirty-seven-year-old public relations executive.

Apart from the tips in the books, what can Executive Mothers do? Well, you can lash out on some eye make-up that makes you look wide awake when you're half-dead. You can arrange a rota with your partner so that you take alternate nights. If you're breast-feeding you could try expressing milk so he can do a night-time feed. If you have a nanny, you can have a system whereby she is on night-call so many times a week, maybe once in the middle of the week and once at the end of the week.

You could also consider two other possibilities. Some babies past the formula stage have an allergy to cow's milk, which can affect their sleep. It's worth trying another sort of milk: ask your health visitor for advice. Other babies, often those who had a traumatic birth, suffer headaches which make them cry and wake. A friend of mine had a very fast second labour and her little boy's head was squashed on his way out. Like many other parents, she found the answer was cranial osteopathy, gentle manipulation of the skull to relieve pressure. If you think this could be the problem with your baby, make sure you use a registered osteopath. You should ring or write to the Osteopathic Information Service (see page 109) for the name of a practitioner.

If things really become dreadful, because your baby cries and cries, don't suffer alone, CRY-SIS runs a helpline (see page 109). When you're at the end of your tether, these women counsellors will help.

'I told my husband I'd bought an egg-timer . . .'
Frantic and funny? One mother I spoke to put the emphasis on fun right from the beginning, even before facing the problem of keeping the windows dry. 'Neither my boyfriend nor I like to hang about. We'd decided on a baby and a baby we wanted. Waiting nine months was bad enough and we couldn't bear the monthly wait to see if, as my Lancastrian mother-in-law puts it, I had "fallen".

'So, one morning on my way to work, I bought an ovulation prediction kit. I wanted to try it straight away, but it suggested waiting until you hadn't peed for four hours. So I tried at lunchtime. Of course, being me, I was trying too early in my cycle, but on the fourth day, it showed positive. Of course, I rang my boyfriend up and we thought "Why wait?" We both had a free lunchtime, so we set off from our offices at different ends of Edinburgh and converged on our bedroom. All very silly, I daresay, but we only had to wait nine months.'

Actually, once the test shows positive, you have two or three days of peak fertility, so going without your lunchtime sandwich isn't necessary. The kits work by measuring the level of Luteinising Hormone in the urine. Luteinising Hormone surges when the egg is mature enough to leave the ovary and prompts the follicle to release it, sending it on its way to the fallopian tube where it waits for the sperm. The surge is around the middle of your cycle, just before you are due to ovulate. Both Clearplan One Step and

First Response include five tests in each packet, enough to cover the vital time in a regular cycle. Both indicate your fertile period with a colour result.

These kits have the edge over the traditional temperature method of pin-pointing the right time of the month, because they tell you when you are about to ovulate, instead of when you have ovulated. The basal body temperature rises by half a degree centigrade after ovulation – a fairly clear indicator once you have monitored your temperature for a while. But it doesn't leave you much time to try to conceive. So the kits are well worth a try for a couple in a hurry, a career woman operating on some pretty fine timing, or a couple having problems conceiving.

'Herod didn't feel guilty. Why should my husband?'
Almost every Executive Mother mentions guilt, either in denying it or admitting to it. 'Why should I feel guilty?' said a few. Why indeed, but more still said they did. There wasn't, incidentally, a single husband who even mentioned the word in relation to himself. In 1993, researchers from Reading University published a survey into working mothers, based on a two-year study of 600 high-earning families in the north-east and the south-east.

Their starting point was thousands of advertisements for nannies, in local papers and in the *Lady*. Demand had doubled in the eighties. More than a third of the women they surveyed employed either a nanny or a cleaner. A substantial number employed both. One of the major interests of the researchers was the class clash between the employer and the employed. Most of the Executive Mothers were not from a background of employing staff in their parental home. Women who were themselves cared for by nannies may approve or disapprove of that for their own children, but are less likely to feel guilty about it than ordinary middle class professional women breaking away from what their mothers did.

'Part of the price I pay is the ketchup bottle on the table.'
One of the researchers, Dr Michelle Lowe, said: 'They felt bad about not looking after their children and had a kind of middle-class guilt about employing someone else to do it.' And often the mother and the 'replacement mother' would disagree over childcare – a warning to get that sort of thing ironed out at the interview stage and written down from day one, as we discussed in the childcare chapters.

Dr Lowe went on: 'The main disputes would be over food and

activities. The nannies were mostly from a lower class background and would be happy to feed them fish fingers and chips, but the parents would want them to eat more healthy "middle-class food" that was freshly prepared. It's a very messy social situation.' Maybe, but if you're firm about what you want from your nanny and fair in your dealings with her, especially about money, time-off and other conditions, you'll make the best of it.

'I could do that!'
Earlier this year, I was invited to a meeting of professional women in Leeds where one of the group was typical of a type of Executive Mother which we should perhaps look at before the book closes, even though some of the preceding chapters probably won't apply to her. She had left her private school at sixteen ('couldn't be soon enough', she said) and had a string of jobs without thinking of a career: clerical, receptionist, telephonist. As she herself put it, if it involved being able to phone her friends, she would have it. A very bubbly and bright woman, she married and had children quite early. It was only then that she started thinking about a career.

Now in her middle forties, she runs a successful recruitment agency. Her formal qualifications were very few and the business is her own, but there are also women with degrees and professional training who have children first and then launch themselves on a career. It takes care of the guilt factor if your children are older when you begin, but it's much harder to climb on to a ladder you've never been on before. A good source of advice is the Working Mothers Association, whose details are in the back of the book.

'I have wash 'n' wear everything: clothes, hair, life. Isn't the female executive a different species from me?'
If you fit into this 'career-later' category and have young children, the chapters on childcare may still apply to you, unless you can wangle your hours round the school day. Many women in this situation, including those who have had a lengthy career break to bring up a family, feel a great lack of confidence. They're not accustomed to wearing smart work clothes and are out of touch with the latest office equipment, they're not used to adult conversation during large parts of the day, and they're used to being in charge of their own domestic world, not to obeying someone else's orders.

It may take a great effort to re-think how you see yourself, but when it comes to job applications, don't dismiss your childcaring years as redundant time-out. Think of the skills you have learnt: timetabling, budgeting, managing, diplomacy. Find me a man who can successfully do in his office day as many things as a home-mother does, and I'll kiss his secretary's feet.

Don't forget all the other things you may have organised: play-groups, mothers' meetings, community work, pressure groups. And you have two great cards to play: maturity and responsibility. Get the most impressive references you can, write off for the WMA's Returners' Pack (see page 109), which is great whether you're returning after a long break or starting for the first time, marshal all your skills on to a curriculum vitae, and go for it.

'I've had five great years at home, which I wouldn't have missed for the world, but another part of me has been on hold all that time.'
I combine home and office in my working life. It's a tightrope, but being a career woman and a mother always is. Some women find a break for full-time mothering is their safety net. One of my colleagues returned to the newspaper three days a week when the second of her sons was ready for playgroup at the age of three. She had returned to work after the first birth, but found she had changed her mind about her priorities. One particular experience when she was reporting from the House of Commons sticks in her mind.

'I had been breastfeeding my baby and had to introduce him to the bottle when my maternity leave ended. Being in the Commons lobby always involves odd hours and late nights, so my husband was in charge of the evening feed. During the sitting, I was tan-noyed. I went to the phone, expecting to hear my news editor's voice on the other end, and instead there was a panicking husband in the foreground and a furious baby in the background. "He won't take this bottle. He just refuses. What do I do?"

'I can hear those yells now. It was a nightmare. I couldn't just walk out of the lobby, so I rang my father and asked him to go round, because he's really good with babies. It turned out that my husband hadn't taken out that little white disc which seals the bottle and prevents leaks, so the poor baby was sucking and suck-ing, but nothing was coming out. No wonder he was frustrated and cross.'

'Anyone know what's in the company handbook about maternity leave?'
The answer to that one has to be a resounding 'no'. I certainly

didn't. More sadly still, none of the women I talked to while preparing this book had done anything to improve her company's maternity deal. No one had been involved in trade union maternity campaigning, for example. It seems that executive women suddenly reach the baby stage of life, turn round and say: 'Right, what's the picture?' and are sometimes disappointed by what they see. There used to be an advertisement which showed a man of around thirty saying 'I'm too young to worry about a pension, right?' The same thing applies to maternity deals.

No one worries about it until it happens to them. One of the problems is that professional women are often not in strong unions; another problem is that we don't want to draw attention to ourselves as potential awkward employees. It's a shame, because individual large employers could do a lot to make motherhood more enjoyable for women, which would make employment with their company more attractive, too. The Working Mothers Association publishes *The Employer's Guide to Childcare*, which is well worth consulting if you do feel a little activism before you decide now is the time for your baby.

'I picked her up at 2 a.m. and she was really hot . . . I couldn't leave her with the nanny.'
This is one we all dread. Your childcare arrangements are going swimmingly: happy child, happy mother. Then illness strikes and you feel as you've never felt before, because leaving a poorly baby who wants you more than she wants anything else is unbearable. When she's well, someone else can keep her safe, feed her and entertain her, but a sick baby isn't interested in being fed or entertained. She wants parental cuddles.

One or two women I know decide parental is very much the operative word and prefer their husbands to take time off work for children's illnesses, simply to avoid giving the impression at the office that they can't be relied upon. The hard fact is that very few employers allow statutory time off to care for sick children.

It's a point of view which may be understandable, but it shouldn't be beyond the wit of a society in which working mothers play a highly trained and highly contributive part to cope with this. One to one, Executive Mothers often find bosses sympathetic, whatever may or may not be written down in the company handbook, but there is still a feeling of a special favour being asked. Some enlightened companies actually allow a number of fully-paid days off each year for caring for dependants (fifteen at Penguin

Books, for example), but more often than not women end up taking holiday.

I find this very unfair. Most professional women could do some of their work at home for a few days and it's well worth ringing up with that suggestion if your child is ill and you are uneasy about leaving her. (Remember, if you have a childminder you can't take an infectious child round to a house full of her other charges anyway.)

If you do decide to try this approach, don't sound as if you're trying to wheedle or beg. Sit down and make a note of anything you may need from the office, then ring up and offer to work from home for a day or two while you look after the baby. Sound positive. 'Amy's ill and needs me. There's some paperwork I can easily catch up on here. Please could one of the juniors be sent round with what I need?'

Keep it brisk and professional. Keep the office in touch with what you're doing, but don't overdo the contact. It only draws attention to your absence and really, in a busy office, no one will be thinking about it half as much as you are. It will come as a great relief to you to know you're with your child and at the same time not deserting your other post. It's not a perfect solution, but it's a much better one than a woman on an assembly line can hope for: she can't offer to do any work from home and she will almost certainly lose a day's pay for a day's caring. Mind you, it's not to be tried on for every infantile snuffle.

'Breast pumps must be designed by men'
Indeed they must. They're a marvellous idea, once you've found the sort you get on with, but there are drawbacks. You stock up milk so someone else can feed your baby while you're at work, but, of course, you also need to pump while you're there. Several women I spoke to returned to work full of good intentions about continuing to breastfeed beyond the end of maternity leave, but were put off by the practical problems of where to pump. Why should we have to use a loo? It's hardly the cleanest place for sterile equipment.

If your company has a nurse, ask her if you can use her room. If not, use the interview room when you know no one is expected or find a sympathetic person who will lend their private office at lunchtime.

But where the male design comes in is the noise these milky contraptions make. Surely a silent pump could be invented? The hand pumps crank and creak; the battery ones whir. The whole thing is fraught with potential embarrassments and the relaxation you need for your milk to flow can be very hard to come by. On the days I'd been to the office, I ended up travelling home on the train after a day's work and milk production with very full breasts, praying that no one would bump into me: it was very painful if anyone did. I wore cream coloured shirts and sweaters for months.

This book started with a look at our changing society and the role of the Executive Mother within it. Women like us are well-placed to influence and change attitudes: not to force all mothers into the workplace but to widen choice for women. Motherhood, executive or not, is too often shortchanged. There's the lack of state help with childcare at one end of the scale; the lack of baby-changing rooms at the other. I've been out for a family lunch at a pub which had won a Peaudouce award, yet had only the broken tiled floor of the women's loo on which I could change my baby's nappy. Elsewhere, I've had a landlord refuse me boiled water for her drink. All too often, motherhood is seen as second-rate, children as a nuisance. Executive Mothers have the best chance to change attitudes for all of us. We are the bods with the bibs and the briefcases and we are here to stay. Even if the bibs occasionally find their way into the briefcases.

Bibliography

Bibliography

Infertility

Getting Pregnant, Robert Winston (Anaya)
Coping with Childlessness, Diane and Peter Houghton
Infertility Services – A Desperate Case, Naomi Pfeffer and Alison Quick
Adopting a Child, by British Agencies for Adopting and Fostering
So You Want to Have a Baby, Serono
Infertility and In-Vitro Fertilisation, Dr Leila Hanna and Dr Elliot Philipp (Family Doctor Publications)
The Infertility Handbook, Sarah Biggs (Fertility Services Management)
Infertility, Your Questions Answered, S. L. Tan and H. S. Jacobs

These titles are available from Issue, whose details are in the address list.

Changing the way you work

Job Sharing: A Practical Guide for Women, by Pam Walton (Kogan Page)
Job Sharing: Putting Policy into Practice
Fair Shares: Making job shares work, by Leighton and Rosen (Hackney Job Share)
The Legal Context to Job-Sharing, by New Ways to Work
Job-sharing introductory pack, by New Ways to Work

The first two titles are available from bookshops. All the titles can be ordered through New Ways to Work, whose details are in the address list.

Our Treacherous Hearts, by Rosalind Coward (Faber & Faber)

Maternity rights

Towards Equality, by the Equal Opportunities Commission. Includes sections on pregnancy and dismissal, job-sharing and part-time work. Available from the EOC, whose details are in the address list.

'Sex Discrimination in Employment', a booklet available free from the EOC.
'A Short Guide to the Sex Discrimination Acts', leaflet free from the EOC.

Childcare

Recent Developments in Childcare, by Peter Mottershead. Available from the HMSO Publications Centre, PO Box 276, London SW8 5DT.
Childcare and Equal Opportunities: Some Policy Perspectives. Available from HMSO.

Pregnancy

Eating Well for a Healthy Pregnancy, by Dr Barbara Pickard (Sheldon Press)
Countdown to a Healthy Baby, by Heather Bampfylde (Collins)
The Good Health Guide for Women, by Jill Turner and Wendy Savage (Hamlyn)
Birth Over Thirty, by Sheila Kitzinger (Sheldon Press)
Down Syndrome: the Facts, by Mark Selikowitz (Oxford Paperbacks)

Sleeplessness

The Sleep Book for Tired Parents by Rebecca Huntley (Souvenir Press)

Useful Addresses

Useful Addresses

Childcare:

Central Bureau,
Seymour Mews,
London W1H 9PE
071-486 5101;

3 Bruntsfield Crescent,
Edinburgh EH10 4HD
031-447 8024;

16 Malone Road,
Belfast BT9 5BN
0232 664418

Immigration and Nationality
Department (for advice about
au pairs)
Home Office,
Lunar House,
Wellesley Road,
Croydon CR9 2BY
081-686 0688

National Childcare Campaign,
Wesley House,
4 Wild Court,
London WC2B 5AU
071-405 5617

National Childminding
Association,
8 Mason's Hill,
Bromley,
Kent BR2 9EY

081-464 6164 and an advice
line on costs on 081-466 0200

Nursery World,
51 Calthorpe Street,
London WC1X 0HH
071-837 7224

Pre-School Playgroups
Association,
61–63 Kings Cross Road,
London WC1X 9LL
071-833 0991

The Lady,
39–40 Bedford Street,
London WC2E 9ER
071-379 4717

Breastfeeding:

Association of Breastfeeding
Mothers,
26 Holmshaw Close,
London SE26 4TH
081-778 4769

La Leche League,
BN 3424,
London WC1N 3XX
071-242 1278

National Childbirth Trust
See *General*.

General:

Active Birth Centre,
55 Dartmouth Park Road,
London NW5 1SL
071-267 3006

Child,
PO Box 154,
Hounslow TW5 0EZ
081-893 7110

CRY-SIS
BM CRY-SIS
London WC1N 3XX
Helpline: 071-404 5011

Down's Syndrome Association,
155 Mitcham Road,
London SW17 9PG
081-682 4001

Equal Opportunities
Commission,
Overseas House,
Quay Street,
Manchester M3 3HN
061-833 9244

Family Planning Association,
27–35 Mortimer Street,
London W1N 7RJ
071-636 7866

Health Education Authority,
Hamilton House,
Mabledon Place,
London WC1H 9TX
071-383 3833

Issue,
318 Summer Lane,
Birmingham B19 3RL
021-359 4887

Maternity Alliance,
15 Britannia Street,
London WC1X 9JP
071-837 1265 and a special line
for the hard of hearing on
071-837 9151

Miscarriage Association,
PO Box 24,
Ossett,
West Yorkshire WF5 9XG
0904 200799

National Childbirth Trust,
Alexandra House,
Oldham Terrace,
London W3 6NH
081-992 8637

New Ways to Work (advice on
job-shares)
309 Upper Street,
London N1 2TY
071-226 4026

The Osteopathic Information
Service
37 Soho Square
London W1V 5DG
071-439 7177

Working Mothers' Association,
77 Holloway Road,
London N7 8JZ
071-700 5771

Index

Index